Testimonials

Taking vows doesn't end the human quest for fulfillment. Spiritual maturity and happiness require integration of sexuality and spirituality. In *Maturing in The Religious Life: The Image of the Heart and the Heart's Desire*, Brother Noel Thomas thoughtfully explores the need specially to express sexuality and love in the context of celibate religious life. In the minds of many, vowed religious life seems to rule out sexual maturity. This book is a very important contribution to those discerning a commitment to religious life, and an invaluable resource for those supporting vowed religious as they seek to live out their commitments as continually evolving and maturing human beings.

Clark Berge SSF,
author of Running to Resurrection: A Soul-making Chronicle.

In *Maturing in The Religious Life: The Image of the Heart and the Heart's Desire*, Noel Jeffs challenges readers to reconsider sexuality and spirituality as interweaving states of being rather than opposing demands. Employing and developing the notion of *maturity*, he argues that the quest to establish an awareness that can acknowledge, and care for, both self and other. At once clearly written and provocative, this is a book that will stimulate heartfelt discussion and meditation.

Professor Ernesto Spinelli,
ES Associates, London UK.

In *Maturing in the Religious Life*, Noel's passion for critical thinking, for questioning norms, and for exploring the meanings of spirituality beyond the strictures of institutional frameworks, emerges boldly. Noel implores us to engage with our 'heart's desire', in this thesis about the relationships between spirituality, sexuality, and indeed, the very essence of being. Why would these ideas not be compelling and intriguing to all of us? While positioned in a rigorous grounding of logic and literature, this provocative work speaks from the heart, pointing to the powerful and unique writing style Noel would go on to develop in his many subsequent works, including so much of his brutally honest contemporary poetry.

Dr Matthew Egan,
Senior Lecturer within the Business School's Discipline of Accounting at the University of Sydney.

MATURING IN THE RELIGIOUS LIFE

The Image of the Heart and the Heart's Desire

This is an IndieMosh book

brought to you by MoshPit Publishing
an imprint of Mosher's Business Support Pty Ltd

PO Box 4363
Penrith NSW 2750

indiemosh.com.au

A catalogue record for this work is available from the National Library of Australia

https://www.nla.gov.au/collections

Title:	Maturing in the religious life
Subtitle:	The image of the heart and the heart's desire
Author:	Jeffs, Noel (SSF)
ISBNs:	9781922703101 (paperback) 9781922703118 (ebook – epub) 9781922703125 (ebook – Kindle)
Subjects:	BODY, MIND & SPIRIT / Sacred Sexuality; RELIGION / Christian Living / Spiritual Growth

Cover concept by Noel Jeffs, SSF

Cover design and layout by Ally Mosher at allymosher.com

MATURING IN THE RELIGIOUS LIFE

The Image of the Heart and the Heart's Desire

Brother Noel Thomas
of the Society of Saint Francis

A Master's Thesis submitted to Antioch University in partial fulfilment of the requirements for the degree of Master of Arts in the Psychology of Therapy and Counselling.

Antioch University London, England

December 1993

Table of Contents

Abstract

I propose that maturity in the context of the Religious Life is the attainment of an identity which transcends and is the tension between an individual person's existence and his or her participation in a social matrix. This is an identity which is capable of experiencing sexuality and adulthood.

It is my contention that religious thinking has found the psychoanalytical view of psychosexual and social development difficult to assimilate and to relate to religious experience and has been antipathetic. The identification of sexuality as both psychosexual and social, and likewise of spiritual development, points to the thrust of my argument that sexuality and spirituality spring from the same roots and that they are not in antithesis.

Both sexuality (in the above terms) and spirituality represent the heart's desire, in their awareness of self and other. This I believe holds the religious pursuit; the creation of a God which is not oneself both sexuality and spirituality contain the desire, which is represented also in fertility, for a recreation of the self. This is paradoxical in that the new life is always different and the past is always unique. It is my contention that when sexuality and maturation in spiritual terms are viewed together, they should be seen as complementary. The spiritual and the social quests are ultimately an expression of the heart's desire.

Introduction

Maturing in the Religious Life involves a spiritual and social quest This is part of a continuing dialogue between individualism and communalism.

I believe this quest is the 'Heart's Desire'. What do I mean by heart? Is this heart the core of our physical being? We know it as an organ of the body. This presupposes another question, 'What body?' Is this the being that I can understand through pain and pleasure, the body whose limits I experience, when I gain an understanding of myself? Is it the body which I know, as relating to ego, and to memory traces; the body onto which memory and experience has thus mapped an ego (Freud, 1927)? It is hard to define where the physical body and the imaginal body begin and end. The imaginal body may be a product of the mature understanding of self, or it may be the body which is experienced as unintegrated and known in terms of memory traces of past times. Life's journey undoubtedly includes a search for a coherent imagery of the self.

This imaging begins as descriptive, and yet it is also an endeavour to portray a physiology in abstract language. We are not speaking of part of the anatomy. It has become part of a symbolic language which includes a loved object and is a record of affects. It has become an imaginative exercise which when the aesthetics are probed, includes a discussion of the self, and a search for truth and knowledge. It may have begun with a simple comment about another person being the heart's desire. We know the heart to be a physical organ and indispensable for the functioning of the human body and human life. We place it on the same level of importance as the mind or mental functioning, and discussions about the presence of life in a person, in both trauma and accident, focus on these two organs. The discussion also focusses on the imaginal thing called the person; the 'I'. The 'I' is a psychic unity, a place of integration and synthesis.

Chapter One
The religious life

We may know the term 'Religious Life' as describing the paths of a variety of people. Are they monastic, or friars or hermits, or those who live enclosed lives in cloisters, or itinerant lives, or work in places of education or caring? They may be known through their 'bloodlines', the charisms of their founders. Are they Augustinians, Franciscans or Benedictines? We may know them in terms of their Rule. Do they follow the Rule of Benedict in the West, or Basil in the East? They may be identified in terms of their ecclesial obedience. Are they Roman Catholic, Anglican, Lutheran or Greek Orthodox? The variety of form and practice may distinguish them. What is their common thread and unity? Many explanations have been provided from within the 'monastic culture'. What is its meaning and theology? Schneiders' reflections on the theology of the Religious Life are useful.

> From the disciplinary point of view, authors have based their theories in scripture, ecclesiology, history, systematic theology, liberation theology and spirituality. What all these attempts have demonstrated is that the richness of the phenomena of religious life and the fecundity of approaching its

> meaning from broader points of view than the dogmatic juridical one that has dominated the theology of religious life at least since the Council of Trent (Schneiders, 1986: 28).

The Religious Life can be seen from a diversity of perspectives. From an Anglican point of view, Allchin (1983) states that there is a unity through the varied forms of the religious and monastic tradition. The premise on which he constructs his argument is that it is a life overflowed into activity, and not an activity supported by a life. Thus he recognises an ideal and a unity, through a temporality which manifests diversity and plurality. His perspective complements Schneiders' viewpoint.

The term 'Religious Life' is used here to denote the practice of living celibate lives within the context of a particular community, with an aim to make and further the notion of a spiritual journey, that journey being a journey of faith. This is its asceticism. The religious community in its journey of faith is characterised by two significant features, the particular sexuality as lived in singular lives, and the vowed life.

McDargh provides a definition of faith which is at the interface of psychology and theology:

> Faith is that human dynamic of trusting, relying upon, and reposing confidence in, which (1) is foundational to the life-long process of becoming a self, and (2) is fulfilled in the progressively enlarged capacity of that self for love and self commitment (1983: 71).

His understanding of 'faith' is that it has goals, and that there is what he terms a quest, 'to – where?'. There is a human development in faith. He names it as love or radical community. He identifies two aspects of this: firstly, the capacity to tolerate ambivalence, and secondly, the sense of oneself as available for loving self-donation (McDargh, 1983: xviii). These address the issues of dominance and submission, and dependence and interdependence.

The sharing in an archetypal story or myth makes the community distinctive in its intention. It also assists the creation of the character of a particular social matrix. The earliest matrix we might experience is of mother or primary caregiver, and baby. S. H. Foulkes, the pioneer of group analytic psychotherapy, said, in speaking of the group matrix, that:

> Looked at in this way ... (it) becomes easier to understand our claims that the group associates, responds and reacts as a whole. The group as it were avails itself now of one speaker, now of another but it is always the transpersonal network which is sensitized and gives utterance or responds. In this sense we can postulate the existence of a group mind in the same way as we postulate the existence of an individual mind (1964).

Matrix is a valuable word for it enlightens the concept of transpersonal. The group has a wholeness and an entity, and may act as a network (Elias, 1991). It raises the philosophical question as to whether the individual precedes the group, or the group precedes the individual. It takes regard of their priority and value. It asks the question whether the individual is born of the group, and gains his or her identity through it. The religious community is not especially delineated as a therapeutic community, though it may function therapeutically. The community or matrix is delineated by its intention and named according to its narrative.

This journey and the community living are overtly recognised by the making of vows which are considered to be both for the individual and the community in the maturational process. The traditional three vows are poverty, chastity and obedience. The individual holds these vows in common with the other members and thus forming a common identity. The profession of vows is the sign of commitment to the life. Schneiders argues that the vows are a later development, and have not always been part of the act of profession, though now they are seen as symbolic of that commitment, and professional as they signify commitment: 'The three vows provide axes around which religious life turns and their profession is a symbolic embracing of that life in its totality' (1986: 66).

The profession is seen as the expression of the encounter with the Divine. Merton (1977: 106) terms the response of the individual as their conversion of manners. This core of the religious vocation is the essence of which the vows are manifest.

The narrative of the group and the social matrix may provide script for any number of people. I believe the two find common ground. In the Christian community, the person extends him or herself by a continual immersion in literature, exhortation and liturgy in 'the Christ Drama'. For some this is called transformation or an exercise in salvation by experience. It is a form of contemplation which is not the result of discursive activity This immersion is called the paschal mystery, or can be merely referred to as the 'Saving Acts of Jesus the Christ'. Boulding says of 'Christian virginity', 'It is not a problem to be solved, but a mystery to be lived and is inseparable from the Easter mystery as a whole' (1982: 27) and Le Clerq: 'Everything comes back finally to a problem of spirituality; what is important is the way in which the way of salvation becomes man's possession in his interior life' (1978: 275). The Religious Life also contains a desire to experience the other, which is also the expression of a separation and individuation process and is more than simply personal enlightenment (Parry, 1980). Rizutto speaks of the first God representation being experienced at the time of this separation: 'It also shows that to create a God that is not oneself. the child has to pass through the glass of mirror to where the real mother dwells' (1979: 187).

The Religious Life is, in theological terms, a manifestation of eschatology, a living of the 'end' and of the ideal. It is an ego ideal where the Christ is the model of the relationship humanity has with the Divine (not necessarily the primal Father), and as an expression of the relationship with all the natural world. The eschatological ideal and virtue of virginity is described by Peter Brown within the context of early Christianity in the Mediterranean.

Marriage was considered essential for the procreation of children, and particularly the procreation of male children. The preaching and advocacy of virginity was viewed as destructive by non-Christians who knew the harrowing inroads of death. It was a drastic renunciation of the moral and social order (Brown, 1990). Contemporary Religious also portray their life as a critique of the current social and moral order (Merton, 1977; Parry, 1980; Morland, 1982; Voillaume, 1978).

Alternatively, some view their lives as a participation and avowal of the created order, an affirming of 'this world' (Boulding, 1982; Schneiders, 1986). The latter speaks of the church's reversal of its view of the world at the time of the Second Vatican Council, a view which now affirmed 'the world'. The relationship of the religious communities to the ecclesial body is described as being radical (where the root of the word is radix, 'the root of'), and yet at the same time they provide a critique. The word 'charismatic' is also used to distinguish the religious within a hierarchical church. The choice of word also identifies them as being non-hierarchical, but also distinctive and yet participatory.

Maturational processes take place within context. These may be the immediate social or societal relationships; they may reflect the individual's history denoting his or her origins whether unique to themselves or held in common with others and identifying those things which might be called characteristic. People find a belonging in their capacity to identify with one another.

Maturational processes can also be designated as those processes which are both healing in their capacities as well as fulfilling, and leading to both greater self-understanding and to developmental goals which have their origins in preceding experiences. Rizutto (1979) argues that theophany and revelation can only build upon the pre-existent object relations.

In a life of faith, there will be developmental periods where vocation will need to be expressed again and renewed, and images of the relationship with the Divine will change and develop.

The relationship of the individual and the Community is the matrix from which both are formed, in their transcending of each other. It is the relationship of 'the one and the many'.

Allchin describes that tension as being 'In the singleness of eternity rather than in the multiplicity of time' (1983: 13). It holds them, and they are the one and the same, a plurality and a unity and also transpersonal. They need not be in opposition to one another, for although each may have their own identity, they can submit to the rule of the other. The common conviction unifies, and is structurally the basis upon which the spiritual endeavours begin. The common conviction is expressed through the aspiration of each individual via the medium of the common life of the group.

The common life is that ability to communicate and particularly to articulate needs and hopes as variants of the common conviction; so that it is expressed in the life of each individual. It requires skills in the articulation of feelings and the sharing of experiences. It may also manifest either a closed system or an open system, as may be found in 'systems analysis'. The open system has provision for 'outlook, feedback and input' (Marteau, 1983; De Board, 1978). This influences its capacity for adaption to changing circumstances, and for the inclusion of new members. Their uniqueness is recognised, and the plurality of the organisation is also given recognition. If there is an organic modelling the organisation will have the ability to remodel itself in changing circumstances. Its authority structure may be overt and hierarchical, or it may be minimalist, horizontal and collaborative. Schneiders describes several models; 'familial, monarchical, democratic, and collegial' in her discussion of authority, rules, and customs (1986: 31). These organisations are rarely without someone who is designated as superior, though 'leaderless' groups do exist.

Religious life is a lifestyle which is intended to foster a dominant interest, which is not only central but absorbing. Its decision-making processes may vary in response to that conviction. Activity may be allowed to precede reflection, or alternatively it may be very hesitant to allow individual movement, beyond that which is authorised, and also reluctant to allow delegation. The religious community may be permissive or conforming and it may fear the polarities of chaos and conformity or order and disorder. It may discourage experimentation. The character of any system may be expressed through its exercise of authority, and in particular its decision-making processes. Marteau's use of open or closed systems analysis is useful here. A group which is able to maintain the dialogue within itself between the individual and the communal might be called a network.

Somewhere a distinction might be made between a community and a society. The former according to the Shorter Oxford English Dictionary (1964) is characterised by the sharing of things in common. It also has common characteristics. Community can be or may be distinguished by sameness, but members of a society acknowledge relationship, and make association. The leaven here seems to be not only in the acknowledging of sameness and things held in common, but also in the recognition of difference. Every member of a society is also or can be a member of a particular community. Form and activity are signs and reflections of the inner process.

Catholic theology discusses the relationship between Grace (the experience of the Divine) and nature: 'Grace builds upon nature'. It asserts that the Divine or supernatural does not subvert or force the natural order in their encounter. The doctrine celebrates the natural order or world of creation and allows for free will as a central tenet of faith and doctrine. The encounter of the Divine with the natural order is one in which the Divine appreciates its character and finitude. The spiritual flows through the common life as a product of this encounter. Marteau makes this argument his premise for contending that in the religious organisation the expenditure of spiritual energies upon a faulty structure is a misdirection of the basic conviction and purpose. The spiritual flows from the Divine encounter with an appreciation of its character through the common life. Meissner (1992), Marteau (1983) and McDargh (1983) all make reference to this doctrine of Grace, with its implications for both the individual and the community. If the common conviction is to be expressed through the members of the group, it ought to follow this path. This is another expression of Allchin' s argument that the activity flows from 'the life' and not the reverse.

A question may be asked as to why a particular community was chosen by someone.

There may not be a response. Communities as regulated groups have conditions of entry. An age of entry would hope to establish that a person has made a free choice and that he or she is legally of age. It is the hope that the person will bring a certain maturity and 'be of their own mind'. It is significant that this style of life is chosen at the point of leaving family. Siblings may have chosen marriage and a sexuality which is procreative. The Religious' choice is a community style of life. The choice of a new matrix will express continuity with the former or even a dissimilarity. This may represent both conscious and unconscious wishes. Why is a religious community chosen? Why is a same single sexuality and a single sex community chosen? Why is a particular authority structure chosen with a 'mother or father', a superior?

These questions return to the intention and the hopes that were inherent within the choice. They speak of desire and the choice of the object.

The new relationship might be hoped to be psychologically healthy, but the health of the community will also play its part. If the community reinforces the pathology of the individual with its own pathology and is not the hoped for relationship in the journey of faith, then external assistance might be required for them both. It is an assumption that the community will be psychologically healthy and the individual not. An institutionalised group can assume a normative role and designate the other as deviant. Groups have a capacity for violence in neglect, abuse, victimisation, and stigmatisation The confidence that when two or three are gathered together 'in my name' can only lead to good might be misplaced evil can also stalk the group (Sandison, 1993). The group may abandon the quest for reality and truth and be seized by 'fear, laziness, greed or omnipotence' (Wescott, 1993: 47) Does the group then become a mob, or a crowd? The pursuit of reality and truth is never easy. Wescott reminds us how rarely religious groups (and even analytic institutions) empower any of their members to march into the unknown,

> for it is noticeable that all heretics and prophets touch upon some truth that the rest of the group is afraid to face, which inevitably leads to their exclusion and often their execution. Scapegoating, which is after all a religious term, is very paradoxical indeed (1993: 47).

Van der Kleij (1993) also speaks of the scapegoat and the desire that we have to murder each other and how then peace is gained by sending that desire into exile. It is by implication that the group has foils to counter its own inherent violence. Violence should not be regarded as something extraneous and to be imported into the group. The desire for power and the fear of change are also characteristic of any group.

The old relationships within family and with kin which coexist with hoped for healing and release may persist in the transference that an individual enacts with a group and its members. The relationships in the new matrix reconstitute the earlier experienced relationships in the matrix of family and its immediate circle, this exemplifying the Freudian observation of the compulsion to repeat. The new may be difficult to begin and relationships difficult to engage. It is the hope of new beginnings and new birth, or new relationships with parental figures or siblings. It is the relationship of the individual, and their community's relationship with him or her. The Religious may have experienced life as being the deviant through being favoured or hated. Emerging from the old environment, and in relationship with 'the new', the person's wish is for self-understanding through their own eyes and the eyes of others. I use the term deviant not in the sense of being abnormal nor as offending, but as providing a social critique by behaviour and lifestyle (Pearson, 1975). Old language and former behaviour may or may not change when placed in the new setting. Alternatively, 'spiritual language' may allow it to be hidden, cloaked, or avoided by disguise for the fear of 'madness' or in fear of change. The 'woundedness' can unveil a new reality. Paradoxically, the 'Achilles Heel' can identify a source of healing. So moves might be made from pleasure to reality with its attendant pain, in an environment which is both secure and holding, and neither fearful nor just containing.

A community may or may not be a container in psychotherapeutic terms. The leader may or may not be able to function this way. The vision and the personality of the leader defines much of the charismatic community through his or her narcissism. Can it be the place of new birth? This is not guaranteed by its structure. Can it be, as in Winnicott's language, 'the good-enough mother'? Can it be the good-enough community? The engagement of the individual within a particular community constitutes, for them both, a new relationship and brings to life questions about self and his or her socialisation.

The transferences that the individual enacts with the new

matrix may allow the discovery and reveal also the transferences and images of God based upon the early object relations. God continues within all stages of life as the transitional object, of one's own creating and also as self-revealing. God belongs to that Winnicottian transitional space, which is the space of play and illusion and the 'resting place' in which we live (Rizutto, 1979). Meissner (1992) similarly makes reference to Ignatius of Loyola's creativity and mystical experience. This transitional space aids the formation of an identity already active within its implicit self-awareness and self-consciousness. It also represents a dialogue with the other in its many and varied forms, thus assisting the formation of a language. Is this language sometimes prayer? It contains and continues our understanding of symbol.

Chapter Two
The concept of maturation

Maturation is a word which is implicit, though not readily used, in psychoanalytic theory. Development and developmental phases gain more attention, alongside the understanding of what is normal and what is real. When used for developmental phases maturation is used descriptively and qualitatively. It is part of the continuing dialogue between the individual and communalism. It poses questions about their interface. It is as though in psychoanalytic theory, the discovery is that in the end, the journey was more important than the dream.

> But you must always *keep* Ithaca in mind. The arrival there is your predestination.
>
> Yet do not by any means hasten your voyage. Let it best endure for many years.
>
> until grown old at length you anchor at your island rich with all that you have acquired on the way.
>
> You never hoped that Ithaca would give you riches.
>
> From 'Ithaca' by C. Cavafy 1863–1933 (Friar 1982: 39).

The word 'developmental' has had greater significance than maturity in psychoanalysis. In the Religious Life 'maturity' is the more prominent word, expressing its concern to be seen as a lifestyle which is authentic and also one of integrity. Religious now express the wish to be seen as adults. We have had a century where we have given birth to, and enshrined, 'the Child' in psychoanalytic terms. Perhaps this has now evoked its complement, 'the Adult'. For Religious one senses

> ... a general commitment ... to their own sexual and affective maturation and to the creation of loving communities which bodes well for the future of religious life. In short my thesis is that all religious have a variety of human, psychological needs, which must be met if religious are to become and function as mature adults and that holiness finds its substrate in such human maturity (Schneiders, 1986: 105, 262).

Schneiders is also concerned to acknowledge spiritual maturity as well, so not leaving 'maturity' as solely belonging to the sexual and affective. In her view, the three areas of need are intimacy, generativity and achievement. She also differentiates spiritual and affective/sexual maturity.

Cintra Pemberton OSH speaks of the intersecting of psychology and theology, asking that this be drawn into the common life or, as she says, 'the everyday stuff of our lives'. She then poses the question, 'Why does all this matter?', and provides an answer:

> Because we are in the business of loving, and we cannot love just in theory – we have to love real live flesh and blood people with whom we live (and some of whom we don't like very much), and we all too often don't do a good job of it. I am convinced that insights into human behaviour are breakthroughs in human knowledge-tools to help us live and love more creatively (1993: 3).

And she posed this against what she saw as the suspicion within Anglican Religious Communities towards psychology.

I have used the work of some significant theoreticians to underline the scope of this dialogue and to see its development in the use of the language of the ego and the self. I commence with Sigmund Freud (1856–1939) and the Freudians, in what I identify as the classical tradition, then look at Margaret Mahler (1897–1985) and Donald Winnicott (1896–1971). I then provide an overview of the work of Erik Erikson (1902–1994) and Carl Jung (1875–1961). Although maturity is sparsely used and seems of little significance in the theory of psychoanalysis, it does seem implicit in the language of psychoanalysis when discussing object-relating and the development of self-representation. This applies to both psychoanalytic theories constructed upon drive theory, and those constructed upon object relations. I find Edith Jacobson's understanding of self-representation useful, as it is linked to identity, and particularly psychic identity.

> I discussed the establishment of self and object representations in the child and their role in the

> building up of object relations, identifications and identity formations. These issues are of the greatest significance for the understanding of psychoses. So are the problems concerning affects and moods (Jacobson, 1971: viii).

A self is understood through both cognitive and affective dimensions, and is not just an awareness of somatic change, variation and modification, as though this were a deviation from the functions of discovery of the apparatus of the mind. Edward Glover (1956) is caustic in making the distinction between a somatic and a psychological maturity. The earlier topographical model, and the later structural models of the mind, were not intended as alternatives but to co-exist.

It is not surprising that in some classifications of psychological theories, psychoanalysis is placed in a position where there is a splitting and reconciling of psyche and soma (Wilber, 1979; 1981). Psychoanalysis reconstructs the history of a person, dwelling on areas of fixation, and its story of developmental sequences of libido and the capacity for sublimation. Juliet Mitchell spells out this reconstruction to allow for the above perspective so the pastiche is seen for what it is. 'It is the way man and women and children "live" themselves in the world.' (1990: 14) Meissner develops and further extends this concept of the economy of libido:

> Thus the Freudian concept of instinctual drives expresses a fundamental fact about the human condition: namely, that man is driven as he is self-

> directing, that he is subject to powerful psychic forces which he also has the capacity to use for his own ends (1992: 353).

Freudian developmental psychology was constructed upon infantile sexuality and the unconscious, and was momentously given birth, with the publication in 1905 of Freud's 'Three Essays on the Theory of Sexuality'. Libidinal development was divided into oral, anal, phallic, latent and genital phases. The Oedipal Complex has its resolution in a person's genital organisation and gender identity. Abraham divided this schema into further subsections 'Maturity, for Abraham, is an emotional relationship with a stable love object with a capacity for a genital- sexual relationship' (Symington,1986:157).

Here maturity and libidinal development are equated. Symington notes that this is different from Freud's view of the individual and society, for here in Abraham's schema harmony reigns between the individual and society. All phases are described in terms of somatic experience. The 'zones' of the body are identified erotically providing pleasure to the person through interaction with him or herself and other people. The child according to Freud was polymorphous perverse (i.e. a bearer of a variety of perversity). His or her entire body is experienced as an erotogenic zone, and through this they find pleasure. It is constructed theoretically upon a primary narcissism, where the baby is able to explore his or her own body and to be the source and sum of pleasure. Taking Havelock-Ellis's word, Freud (1905) designates this phase as auto-erotic and as one which will not be repeated until after the latency period.

In theorising, primary narcissism became the ground of religious experience. We can relate this to Freud's own experience, and to Meissner's study of Ignatius of Loyola, in which he equates an 'infinite resignation' within and beyond the 'oceanic experience'. Meissner utilises Soren Kierkegaard's concept of the infinite resignation (Meissner, 1992; also McDargh, 1983) to describe the state experienced after moving out and beyond the primary narcissism This becomes comparable to both Erikson's basic trust, and Lacan' s 'wish of wish fulfilment' (Owen 1993). It contains desire, but it also has resigned infantile wish fulfilments. 'It returns to trust to go beyond it' (Meissner 1959: 56).

The 'oceanic experience/feeling' arises in the correspondence of Freud and Romain Rolland in 1927. Rolland had responded to Freud's discussion of an experience that he had on the Acropolis in *The Future of an Illusion.* Freud (1930) dedicated *Civilisation and its Discontents* to Rolland.

> This he says consists in a peculiar feeling which he himself is never without, which he finds confirmed by many others, and which he supposes is present in millions of people. It is a feeling which he would like to call a sensation of 'eternity', a feeling as of something limitless, unbounded – as it were oceanic (1930: 64, 65).

Margaret Mahler in her schema likens the oceanic experience to a normal symbiosis where an omnipotent system exists: 'a dual unity within one common boundary' (1991: 44). Wisdom (1970) also makes reference to this oceanic feeling:

> The broad picture of primary narcissism is one of self feeling – not even concern for one's self, for no contrasting other is recognised as such. The problem for the infant and for Freud's libido theory is how to burst the dam of narcissistic libido and attach one's feelings to another (1970: 343).

John Rickman (1957) treats this same oceanic feeling with an enthusiasm, as the source of spirit and creative ecstasy.

The transition from primary to secondary thought processes and the move from pleasure to reality undergird the theorising of libidinal development and primary narcissism. The libidinal or developmental phases which are categorised as belonging to the infantile may bear fruit in any part of life when the complexity of the infantile within the adult through the unconscious processes asserts itself: 'Achille's self seeking consciousness resolves that moment and the moment of our infantile experience in the notion of self consciousness itself' (MacCary. 1 982: 27).

This recognition is an expression of the correlation of the present with an understanding of the past in any current trauma or incident. The infant remains as a part of the adult, even though this is a schema which ties development to various ages with transitional phases. From this perspective 'this child' is platonic, and is a reconstruction. The questions that arise within this model, are those of fixation along this developmental schema, and of sublimation, with a person's growing awareness of their own history.

Freedom from repression, which leads to sublimation or aim

inhibition of sexuality and to genital organisation is regarded as being possible in three ways. First, repression is replaced by a condemnatory judgement so the person is rid of the earlier consequences. The second is an employment in useful purposes so that the energy of the infantile wishes are not cut off. Those which Freud called the original unserviceable aims, are being replaced by one(s) that are higher, and perhaps no longer sexual. This is not intended to designate those instincts as neutralised, but as de-sexualised (Sandler & A. Freud, 1985). 'It is probable that we owe our highest cultural successes to the contribution of energy made in this way to our mental functions' (Freud, 1974: 85). The third of the possible outcomes is experienced as satisfaction of the now conscious wish. We have again met the interface of the personal and the social. The changes between pleasure and unpleasure are enforced by reality and mark the quest which Freud describes as being often too difficult for humans to bear, one from which they make their retreat. It is, as Ogden (1986, 1990) acknowledges, the continuing dialectic between the unconscious and the conscious and the changing foreground. Brown's study of sublimation contains the following synopsis:

> Freud's two instincts – Eros and Death – are fundamental hypotheses as to the general character of the repressed forces inherent in human nature by virtue of its connection with a body. Though repressed and unrecognised. these are the energies which create human culture. and to recognise their existence is to reinterpret human culture. Human

> culture is then reconnected with the human body. Eros creates culture, and Eros is the bodily sexual instinct (1970: 21).

This places the Freudian psychosexual developmental pattern within the dialogue of the individual and communalism.

Object relating is not the exclusive property of the Object-Relations school within psychoanalytical thought. Wisdom in his study of Klein and Freud clarifies the relationship as he sees it:

> To avoid misunderstanding it must be emphasised that Freud included a vast quantity of object-relational explanation in his scheme ... man is a being whose object relations can be swamped by biological sexual drives: for Melanie Klein, man is a being whose sexuality is object-relational from the first cry to the death rattle (Wisdom,1979: 340).

This description of Freud again picks up Meissner's (1992) perception of the man or woman as driven and also self-directing. The baby's first environment is constituted by his or her primary caregiver, who is also his or her first object or part object. Freudian theory is constructed from the primary narcissism and the instinct or drive gratification. There is always a regressive pull even for the adult. Freud made the distinction that there is an anaclitic and a narcissistic choice of objects. The first reproduces a pre-existing object-relationship and the latter, an object relationship on the model of the subject's relationship to his or herself (Laplanche & Pontalis, 1988). Edward Glover in his expositions of classical Freudianism was to point out that instinctual drives and their aims always take precedence over object recognition. But Glover was also to point out, 'in the postulation of a greater number of stages in object formation, we had one further means of distinguishing a greater number of ego stages' (1968:39). Glover's focus was on ego psychology and the structural position, and it was through papers over a number of years that he drew together the idea of a nuclear hypothesis for the birth of the ego. He drew a correlate which was almost an intentionality between ego and object. He utilised Janet's concept of disassociation in order to elucidate why there was ego strength or ego weakness at any particular stage of life. He also contested the development of Kleinian ideas, when he said,

> The completeness of an object depends upon the wholeheartedness of instinctual aims. The only senses in which early pre-genital objects are part objects is in so far as libidinal strivings are polymorphous 'the term part object is after all an object's view of an object … The ego's libidinal relation to its objects is also in the process of forming object images … Any psychic system which (a) represents a positive libidinal relation to objects or part objects: (b) can discharge reactive tension (i.e. aggression and hate against objects and (c) in one or other of these ways reduces anxiety, is entitled to be called an ego-system or ego nucleus Thus an oral system gratifies instinct on a part object

> (mother's nipple), it can exert aggression towards the nipple (sucking, pulling, biting) and is able to prevent some degree of anxiety. This is the model or prototype of an independent, autonomic, primitive ego nucleus (1968: 31).

His construct included, as well as ego development and object recognition, super ego formation. The latter is a result and culmination of the process where introjection of the primary objects is the ground for the super ego formation. Nevertheless, in this context object images are also made of the self in cathexis and are endopsychic.

Whereas I have used Glover's expositions to explore this point, Masterson's (1981) critique of Kohut is also enlightening. He argues that the evidence of child observation tends to confirm the reciprocal interrelatedness of the development of the self and of object relations as outlined by Freud in 'Instincts and Their Vicissitudes' (1915), and 'On Narcissism; an Introduction' (1914). These defining an initial relationship, and the linking of self and object, and then their separation. 'This separation is followed by progressive, separate, parallel maturation of both self and object representations, mutually influencing each other' (Masterson, 1981: 20).

Janet Sayers asserts the significance of changes in character which developed in psychoanalysis through the work of Anna Freud. She also points out the relationship between the subject and the object. between ego and its objects and their correlating development. Sayers says of Anna Freud: 'In detailing the developmental line towards internalising the parent as a real figure, Anna also described the line from neglect to care of the body' (1991: 186). This was placed in the context of maternal deprivation, and a corresponding premature development. When Rizutto makes her study of the concrete entities of objects and object representations, she remarks upon them as capable of attracting the individual's wishes and becoming preconscious; in a way which is comparable to Anna Freud's theorising.

> They also have the power to colour all future relations of the individual, and most specifically the relation to the analyst and its concomitant affectual experience. They can exert power over the individual and cause him to experience powerful emotions, whether in the historical re-encounter of the primeval father in the Sinai, or the equally intense reawakening of the parents 'in the flesh' in transference. Both give the impression that the representation has power of its own (1979: 63).

She is pursuing a path which would take us further into the school of object relations.

Here, as I have endeavoured to portray it, is object relating in the psychoanalytic area which diverges from a pattern of maturing as though maturing was the arrival at a psychosexual genital level of organisation. Maturing is permitted to continue in different circumstances, and at different times through object relating. Ogden making a distinction between Freudian object relations and the School of Object Relations, notes that there is a real interaction with actual external objects and that a process of internalisation takes place, and that the early object is not predominantly created by the infant (1991). MacDougall (1990: 301) speaks of the self-representation as being in eludibly linked to the necessity for 'man's young to come to terms with the reality trauma of the other.' This language has its basis in Freudian narcissism. Although she describes the personal identity as an illusion and also as a reality without contradiction, she sees it as being of primordial need in the individual's psychic life as though it were a struggle against psychic death.

> The self-representation is based on an intricate interpenetration of the libidinal investments of the self with those of the inner and outer objects, intricate intermingling of the narcissistic and the libidinal economy, a mutual pact which is ceaselessly renewed (1990: 302).

This discussion, begun through Freud, interpreted by Glover and with the help of others, has brought us to a stage of exploring some relationship between ego and self.

Edith Jacobson in her studies of psychosis. object relating and inner object loss reflects:

> Whereas the central fear of the neurotic is castration fear, the psychotic is afraid of an impending dissolution of the psychic structure-involving a partial or total breakdown of object and self-representations and resulting in a withdrawal from

> the external world to the point of manifest psychotic symptom formation (1967: 17).

When Jacobson (1965) addressed the issue of the ego, the self, and self-representation in an individual's object relating, in that person's selective object identification she wrote:

> They refer to the ambiguous use of the term ego; i.e. to the lack of distinction between the ego which represents a structural mental system, the self, which I defined above, and the self-representation. Hartmann (1950) called attention to this point-suggests the use of the latter term (analogous to object representativeness) for the unconscious, pre-conscious and conscious endopsychic representation of the bodily and mental self in the systems ego. I have worked with this concept for years, because I have found it indispensable for the investigation of psychotic disorder (1965: 18).

The development of Object Relations theory on both sides of the Atlantic placed theories of development more firmly within the mother-child or primary caregiver and child relationship. The baby's and infant's mental development begins not only as the development of drives, but as object related and environmentally placed. Margaret Mahler and Donald Winnicott have both explored this area in their own ways. Winnicott bears the benchmark of Melanie Klein, and the English Object Relations school. Margaret Mahler's work on the symbiotic development of children in the mother and baby relationship continued within the ambits of classical Freudianism. Her work is based upon a study of the pathology of psychotic children and with a view to seeing those steps which preceded and influenced the Oedipus Complex. Thus she bound herself by the constraints of classical Freudian theory. She is also the scientist who made this her study. She made consistent reference to Edward Glover and to Edith Jacobson for support and clarification of her own work.

Mahler in 1952 first used the concept of symbiotic psychosis, and then sought to apply this in terms of the normal development of the child. She was concerned that her readers should see the mother-child matrix as the crucial area. The gratification of instinct for the child comes through the mother or primary caregiver. She described the mother as 'the symbiotic organiser, and the midwife of individuation, and of psychological birth' (1991: 47). She also said 'like any intrapsychic process this reverberates throughout the life cycle' (1991: ix), and may never be finished. There was an expectation that new derivatives of the earliest processes could still be seen at work. They sometimes required resolution at a later time in a person's life in an unresolved sense of self-identity and body boundaries. These derivatives could be reactivated or remain peripheral to the person. Freud wrote of the body ego, and Glover of mental apparatus, but Mahler is in a way comparable to McDougall, when she uses the expression of 'body'. McDougall uses the term psychosomatic, so defining 'the body' as an experiential relationship between psyche and soma. The body is also the concern of Edith Jacobson in her use of the concept of self-representation.

Mahler (1991) developed her theory using three concepts: separation, symbiosis and identity, all which she described as being intrapsychic. The first was a self-representation which was distinguished from representations of the object world. Symbiosis was intrapsychic, and not to be postulated in behavioural terms. It was a feature of cognitive-affective life.

Identity she describes in terms of the statement, 'that I am'. It was the earliest awareness of a sense of being when there was a cathexis of the body with libidinal energy. The title which she gave to her book, indicates a recognition that there are two births of an infant. The first is the natural and physical birth, and the other is a psychical birth. Physical maturation is perceived as being more or less built in and proceeding automatically, whilst psychological development is not. These are quite separate events, and there is no expectation that the phases of development will coincide at the same time in any two children.

> We find it instructive to compare children who were slow in locomotor development with precociously walking toddlers. For example two of our little boys were at the opposite ends of the spectrum of the two tracks of the separation-individuation process: maturation versus development, separation versus individuation. The one came to us already walking at the age of nine months: the other took his first unaided steps only two days before he was seventeen months-fully eight months apart! (1991: 64).

And from there she went on to explain this discrepancy.

The phases of development as she perceived from her research were pre-symbiotic, symbiotic and separation-individuation. This allowed her to focus on the development of object relations and restoration of missing or distorted maturational and developmental ego functions. She delineated four consecutive and overlapping subphases in the process of separation-individuation: differentiation, practicing, rapprochement, and the last and culminating phase, which is open ended. At the same time libidinal object constancy was achieved gradually along with the consolidation of individuality, and the basis for gender differentiation was laid down. In the last phase the self has become differentiated from the object and is known internally and known as the self-representation.

The goal of this developmental plan is 'the normal adult', who has achieved a separation from the world out there, and yet is able to be fully in it as well as fully out of it. This achievement is normally completed within the first three years of life. At each stage the transition may be achieved easily or traumatically. In its entirety it becomes the significance of being, and becoming separated and experiencing the state of separation.

I tum to Winnicott now whose analytic observations compare favourably with the research data of Mahler. They are similar in their emphasis on the mother-child relationship but each moved in different directions. His emphasis on the mother-child relationship earned him the title of the 'quintessential matriarch' (Sayers,1991: 264). He was able through this perspective and through the exploration of 'mirroring' which occurs between the child and the parent figure in their facial contact to address also the separation and individuation processes. He also explored the recognition of sameness and difference. which arises in this early two-persons experience. Many concepts have come down to us through him, but if left to stand alone they are meaningless. What is the good-enough mother? What is the capacity to be alone? What is the Transitional Object? What is the False Self? What is Mirroring? All of these are contributions to psychoanalytic thought from Winnicott. These concepts all contain paradox as though life is always a play between two poles. His writing belongs to that period between 1920 and 1970. He had been analysed by James Strachey and Joan Riviere. Melanie Klein supervised his work with children.

He worked as a paediatrician for forty years and it was through his work with children that he came to be recognised. He differed from Klein in that he viewed the psychological development of the child as arising from the dependence on the mother whereas she viewed the child as a distinct entity from birth. He is comparable to Mahler, in noting the distinction between a physical birth and a psychological birth. Both Mahler and Winnicott carry the influence of Edward Glover's thought on integration of the ego. For Winnicott the first phase of a child's life was an unintegrated phase. He saw that maturity was something to be achieved and that integration was a phenomenon only to be arrived at through and from an unintegrated state. The baby could achieve integration of a self even momentarily and then when relaxed returned to the unintegrated state. The integrated self was to be achieved later and was desired as it brought the reward of object relating. His work laid a new emphasis on the facilitating environment. Holding became a significant term which expressed the capacity to identify with the baby and to be empathetic. It was a concept which was transposed into the psychotherapeutic world. He was noted for his willingness to allow patients to regress into pregenital sexual levels of development and then to recommence developmental processes. He said:

> In an environment that holds the baby well enough, the baby is able to make personal development according to the inherited tendencies. The result is a continuity of existence, that becomes a sense of existing, a sense of self, and eventually results *in* autonomy (1990: 280).

This began with the paradoxical expression that it was not possible to describe an infant without describing a mother. The facilitating environment meant that the interpersonal was more important than Kleinian 'Phantasy'. It was not to underplay the significance of the biological maturation but to place it in the context of the actual experience of the psychological matrix. He felt that development was a natural and inherent process. Biology and psychology were inseparable and were parts of the same process of development. The process was always a relationship: 'Although in health the adult continues to grow, develop and change right up to the moment of death' (1988: 7). Winnicott explored the relationship of health and maturity:

> The built in tendency to recover links depression also with the maturation process of the individuals

> infancy and childhood, a process which (in a facilitating environment) leads on to personal maturity, which is health (1986: 72).

Socialisation is the harbinger of this maturity: 'health of the psyche is to be assessed in terms of emotional growth, and is a matter of maturity' (1988: 12). His usage of the term maturity is more than a definition in terms of genital organisation and genital activity. His use of the words psyche and soma create an endopsychic framework, distinguishing a new relationship with 'mind'. His theoretical constructs contain the Oedipus Complex and he utilised the Freudian erotogenic zones of development. He believed that 'the abnormal always points to the normal' (1988: 50). Winnicott's presentation of his dynamic psychology is in the following way:

> a) Interpersonal relationships and attendant complications
> b) The achievement of a personal unit and the capacity for concern
> c) The primitive tasks of
>   1. Integration of the self
>   2. Psycho-somatic *modus vivendi*
>   3. Reality contact through Illusion
>
> (1988: 35).

It is a presentation of the primary world of the child, which is at the core of his schema of human development. This world is the one that the child has created with the mother. This facilitating environment, is one which she enables through her primary maternal preoccupation. She is a creation of the child, meeting his or her every need. 'Need' is the essential word here in contrast to the Freudian desire and wish. The good-enough mother who is content to provide this narcissistic environment in which there is both a primitive psychological organisation and a relatively mature one creates this illusion. This experience though, may only be for a short time. This is the stage of mirroring. It is an adaption which in time the mother or primary caregiver also fails to maintain for one reason or another and then the baby has a disillusionment. Thus the baby learns what it is to desire, in his or her need for gratification. In this adaption he or she is frustrated in their instinctual wishes.

These developments contain a sequential passage from oneness to separation as the baby authors his or her experience. Here is the discovery of the 'not-me'. The phases of development are constructed upon each other each frustrating the other. This rearrangement of the adaptive process is also the ground for anger and disillusionment and guilt and the development of concern. The failure of the facilitating environment is also the ground for a pathological development of a compliant and adapted self which Winnicott terms the false self (Winnicott, 1989; Masterson, 1981). The nature of the object is central to his thinking. Once the child has discovered that the mother figure has not been destroyed and that she has her own continuity and being, he or she begins the process of discerning both internal and external reality. Winnicott says, 'The development of the capacity for concern is therefore a complex affair. and it depends on a continuing personal relationship between and infant and a mother-figure' (1988: 73).

In this experience of differentiation the transitional object represents the mother in its sensible, concrete and tangible qualities. Its significance is symbolic as it marks the passage towards internalisation. The internalisation is not of the object itself but of the object as an environment. It is a new space, and a creative space for living, and it recalls the experience of the capacity to be alone, and alone in the presence of another; 'the child must have the opportunity to play alone in the presence of the absent mother, and in the absence of the present mother' (Ogden, 1990: 182). The mother's role as the invisible co-author was taken on by the child in this creation of internal space. 'Illusion creates the object world in a particular way. and it also acknowledges that our subjective understanding of facts is through the medium of illusion' (Syminton, 1990: 318).

Transitional space involves the continued exploration and creation beyond our internal world recognising that we create our own world of objects.

Erik Erikson was analysed by Anna Freud. Sayers records that Anna infuriated him by knitting in the analytic sessions though she did at least give him some jumpers for his children (1992: 160, 281). He trained in Vienna and then returned to his native America. He was significantly influenced by the works of Anna Freud (1936, *The Ego and the Mechanisms of Defence*) and H. Hartmann (1939, *Ego Psychology and the Problem of Adaption*) on ego psychology. Anna Freud's theorising provided him with the concept of an average adult (Erikson, 1982, 1985: 8). Erikson (1982) argued that adulthood is the link between the individual lifecycle and the cycle of generations. His work allied a psychosocial development in relationship to the original Freudian schema of psychosexual development. A further development of his theorising has been to relate questions of identity to personality and adulthood. At every phase of development, he conceptualised significant psychosocial development within the context of social development and the differing radii of communal experience.

This study evolved from a study of his own identity and the experience of the American identity when it had been tested by events and trauma larger than itself (1959, 1980: 44). His work is the study of ego psychology at a communal level as begun by Freud in 1921 which was built upon the concept of primary narcissism. In 1936, at the same time as Anna Freud had published *The Ego and the Mechanisms of Defence* he and fellow American R. Spitz, both interested in social anthropology, had visited the Sioux community (1982, 1985) From that experience of the relationship of the economy of the individual and the ecology of the community he said:

> Training in such groups, soon we concluded is the method by which a group's basic ways of organising experience (its group ethos: as we came to call it) is transmitted to the infants early bodily experiences, and through them to the beginnings of his ego (1982, 1985: 23).

This experience seems comparable to the Freudian concept

of the ego as a body ego. The approach is comparable to that which Erikson took in dream analysis. Kernberg (1992) records that in 1954 Erikson's focus was on the increasing importance of the expressive and the interactional in contrast to the directly symbolic. The interpersonal was being stressed more than the intrapsychic.

Erikson (1982, 1985) pointed out that in a human being's existence and the development of personality the somatic, the psychic process and the communal were significant. He defined these firstly in terms of a hierarchic organisation of bodily organ systems and then as dealing with ego synthesis and finally with cultural organisation and ethos. An overview of the chart is required, with its eight stages. Brown and Pedder have divided the eight segments into a first five and then a second grouping of three. The five they consider as having an equivalence to the Freudian psychosexual phases, and the three, they consider to be comparable to Jungian stages of development. This cycle and chart of development is popularly used in relationship to the phases of Freudian psychosexual development, providing a psychosocial comparison (Brown & Pedder, 1979, 1981: 39; Rizutto, 1979: 206–207). Both place it in parallel charts. Erikson is the precursor to Bowlby who in 1958 developed his work on *Attachment and Loss* using ethological studies (Massie & Rosenthal, 1984). The cycle of development which longitudinally saw a development from childhood in old age until preparatory to death, had not detached and separated childhood

The Eriksonian life cycle has the following stages marked by antitheses of satisfactory and unsatisfactory adjustments. It is constructed upon the antitheses of trust and mistrust (oral), autonomy and shame and doubt (anal), initiative versus guilt (phallic and Oedipal), industry versus inferiority (latency), identity versus identity diffusion (early and late adolescence), intimacy and generativity versus isolation and self-absorption (adulthood), and finally integrity versus despair (senescence and death). I have used Rizutto's 'charting' to show the relationship and comparison of Erikson and Freud (Rizutto, 1979: 206–207). Erikson later asserted that the resolution of each antithesis or crisis brought forth a virtue. Out of the antithesis of trust and mistrust could arise the virtue of hope (1982, 1985) That hope might be seen and acted out from a religious perspective or alternatively a person might seek another resource. Using Erikson's perspective and charting, there could be a reconstruction of childhood from any subsequent data even when the early data was missing. The chart was dependent upon the concept of an 'epigenetic development':

> Whenever we try to understand growth, it is well to remember the *epigenetic principle* which is derived from the growth of organisms *in utero*. Somewhat generalised, this principle states that anything that grows has a ground plan, and that out of this ground plan the parts arise, each part having its time of special ascendancy, until all parts have arisen to form a functioning whole (1968, 1983: 92).

He goes on to describe this organically based process as one which is propelled forward and of which we become aware. In this process we interact with an extending radii of people. This development of personality has both upward drives and outward movements into ever widening or varied circles. Every centre of epigenetic development continues to expand and develop through life. The phases are built upon age specific tasks each having its own appropriate and adequate ritual of passage.

Erikson asked the question as to whether 'pregenitality' existed only for the development of genitality. That question was partially answered by the subsequent usage of 'basic trust' in psychoanalytic circles, as a measure of suitability for analysis (Etchegoyen, 1991). A second of his concerns was whether ego synthesis was only for the individual. Did it have wider implications in terms of ethos and of communal activity? His description of the levels of development was of a succession of potentialities; not a mere succession, but of potentialities which could be resolved for good or for ill. The child's erotic experiences which gave rise to sexual and genital primacy were in puberty but they also contained a usage which was for social modalities. From these experiences arose appropriate ritual and meeting. At puberty there was a discovery of the object within the reconciling of the paradox of the one and the other. The other could also be the numinous. The ego provided a space-time experience and within the context of a life-plan the capacity for 'play' furnished adaptability. The source of each individual's beginnings began in their group identity. The following quote from Erikson pertains to the Sioux but reflects these thoughts about the relationship of the individual and the community: 'We pointed out that the identities of these groups rested upon extreme differences in geographical and historical perspectives (collective ego. space-time) and on radical differences in economic goals and means (collective life plans)' (1959, 1980: 20).

He developed this to say that the process preserved the social typology of the beginnings and also the outline of the body image (1959, 1980). He brought into play the preservation of communitarian values and identity and also the establishment of the individual's endopsychic identity. The quest to discern sameness and difference become significant when there is meeting and the construction of ritual.

What does this theorising furnish for ego psychology and self psychology? The significance which Erikson highlights in the constructing of an identity is not only its intrapsychic development but also in the awareness of the interpersonal: 'the immediate perception of one's self sameness and continuity in time; and to the other simultaneous perception that others recognise one's sameness and continuity' (1959, 1980: 23). The intrapsychic is recognised as an expression of subjectivity. The 'I' as a sensory and thinking creature is held in confrontation with the self and yet whilst in relationship to a 'we'. There is not just one self, but a number of selves. This is a reminder of Edward Glover's concept of the ego nuclei and its multiple faces. The ego in this construct becomes an unconscious ego which adapts and synthesises and the person has a sense of being, 'centred and active. whole and aware and overcoming a feeling of being peripheral. or inactivated … fragmented and obscured. The person has an 'I' and a 'self' (1982, 1985: 86).

The work of Carl Gustav Jung is usually seen in relationship to Freud. Their relationship, was indeed complex. It is easy to name a date as to when they broke with one another and went in their divergent ways after they had shared much and encouraged each other. It is an oversight to see them as having been together theoretically. As N. O. Brown states, 'Ontogeny recapitulates phylogeny (i.e. each individual recapitulates the history of the race)' (1959, 1970: 13). This overview contains their different perspectives within the question of an individual's relationship to his or her community. Freud insisted upon the centrality of sexuality and drive theory in the individual whereas Jung focussed on the mythology of humanity's existence to provide the understanding of the individual's meaning and consciousness. It was the question of the collective unconscious, which marked their separation and drew out their differing views of the individual and the group. Samuels (1989: 3) describes analytical psychology and psycho-analysis as sibling disciplines. (Perhaps that is another way of describing Jung and Freud as rivalrous siblings.) Both are termed depth psychologies, having in common the notion of the unconscious. When Jung first sought a name for his work, he used 'complex psychology', but later named his work analytical psychology. His interest was not in just the mind or mental activity. He preferred the word psyche instead of mind. The psyche also contained the unconscious. For him the highest attainment was that of the development of personality 'whereby an individual becomes as complete a human being as it is possible for him or her to be.'

This was the actualisation of the self The self stood at the core of this construct in an axis with the ego. With this model

Jung differed markedly from psychoanalytical theory. The core, and the archetype of archetypes was the self in the collective unconscious, which is coterminous with the natural world. In the same way that drive theory of Freudian theory found its basis in the biological order. Stevens notes that the psyche was viewed as part of nature and had a biological basis. Thus any one person's life story was to become confessionally the story of the self-realisation of the unconscious. The collective unconscious was the heart of this model. In occasions of regression (which were an essential part of a developmental process), the self is the centre beyond which it is impossible to go. Jung's work at the Burgholzli Asylum with schizophrenia is the context within which to view this theorising. The ego which is in the axis with the self and mediating the self with the world and the world with the self, is marked by the persona, which is a social face for the many different contexts and experiences it experiences. Libido as a vital physic energy may be the source of various energies and not to be seen as just sexual. Jung differed from Freud in his view of incest, seeing it not only as sexual but as symbolic of the spiritual. The complexes of the personal unconscious functioned beyond the reach of the conscious will and possessed their own ego, having also persona, shadow, will, anima and animus. It was a reminder that environment did not grant personality.

The psyche is a self-regulating system, using the principles of homeostasis. It is comparable to Hegelian thesis, antithesis and synthesis. Wholeness is the quest for individuation and is viewed teleologically. All life, which includes personal development, is a balancing act between the personal and the collective, 'through which each of us sustains his or her version of those universal regulations which govern all of humanity' (Stevens, 1990, 1991: 54). The life cycle is thus regarded as a whole, and psychological changes are genetically determined. The phases are marked by transition and rite. Within each transition, there are the processes of separation, transition and incorporation. The first two phases of this life cycle are biological and social and the last two are cultural and spiritual. This is termed maturation, whereas psychoanalysis viewed it as normality with the experience of development as a comprehension of reality. Individuation means precisely the better and more complete fulfilment of collective quantities which are invested in the self. Health is that desirable state when archetypal needs are met in outer fulfilment through the ego.

Jung's work was implicitly based around the mother and infant while the Oedipal Complex was of little significance to him.

Chapter Three
Conventional views of the place of sexuality in the religious life

Is there a conventional view of the sexuality of the Religious Life from the point of view of both the outsiders and those who live the life? Amongst the popular images of the Religious Life must surely be Julie Andrew's portrayal in *The Sound of Music* (1965); a romanticised biography of the Von Trapp family living through the vicissitudes of World War Two. It is the paradigm of the nun or sister who leaves her desert, and who finds fulfilment in a heterosexual partnership and care of children. It contains unspoken implications about the life of 'the convent-desert' and the value placed upon heterosexual marriage and family. The value systems are set beside one another. The Religious Life remains enigmatic and a puzzle. In 1959 Audrey Hepburn featured in *The Nun's Story*. It is not surprising to find books such as Bernstein's *Nuns* (1976, 1979), and Loudon's *Unveiled. Nuns Talking* (1992) on library shelves, or *The Brides of Christ* (1992–93) as television viewing and on the shelves of the bookshop, Maitland's, *Virgin Territory* (1984, 1993). Ardetti's *The Celibate* (1993) represents the alternate story for men. The same question is asked; whether self-discovery can be other than through the body and its passions.

There is always a market for the mystery. The mystery invites speculation about illicit or covert and confusing sexuality. We may note the interest shown in the film *Agnes of God* (1985) or even in the Sisters of Perpetual Indulgence of the 'homosexual community'. The interest in 1992–93 of trials of the Christian Brothers in the United States and Australia for child abuse in their schools, or the Irish bishop who was a source of scandal in his dealings with a mistress and his illegitimate child, recognise that sexuality in the Religious Life can be the food for scandal and the meat of the popular press. It provokes questions about the place of sexuality in the Religious Life, firstly as scandal, and then if people are willing, as the ground for further reflection.

Nuns on the Run (1990) and films which place the escapades of men within the convent and in nun's habits, make inferences about the ease of crossdressing in the environment of the convent and invite questions about the sexuality of the convent's inhabitants. It is not surprising that when Geoffrey Moorhouse writing about the enigma, titled his book *Against all Reason,* or that Schneiders' theology is about *New Wineskins.* The latter arises from the Biblical parable of the impossibility of containing unfermented wine in old skins. Just what can be contained and what is containable? Sexuality has a pungent odour. The question of bodies and their sexuality as part of a whole, invites exploration.

In a conventional view no distinction is made between sensuality and sexuality. No difference is recognised between non sexuality and celibacy as though this permanent chastity is an absence. of sexuality. Permanent continence is seen as a non-sexual life. Celibacy is contrasted with genital relationships and they are not seen as comparable in any way.

Questions about the utilisation and diversion of sexual energy suggest that this is somehow sublimated in work and industry and altruism. Distinctions are made about love and genital sexuality, as though through the experience of a celibate's life the truth of the former is preserved. Love thus being considered a virtue and a truth is considered to have a greater power than sexuality (Cotter, 1977).

The experience of the married or non-celibate is that chastity is part of their life as just as much as genital sexuality. Solitude is also characteristic of marriage and partnership as is companionship. These characteristics are shared by both celibates and non-celibates alike and cannot be used to distinguish them apart. Marriage requires more than love for its foundation (Den Haag, 1964).

The Desert Fathers, who in their theology emphasised the single mindedness of 'the heart' as 'the open heart', often faced famine and starvation in their agrarian culture. They mobilised in the name of spirituality the physical person as a whole. The ache of fasting counted for more than the sexual drive so their desert asceticism gave recognition to the drives of hunger before sexuality (Brown, 1990). Those who went into the desert would have already known sexual renunciation as part of the contemporary Christian culture. It was characteristic of their parents' lives. This renunciation would not have represented a greater virtue to them whereas the limitation of food would have. Schneiders (1986: 137) picks up this theme when she reflects: 'Without sex, one does not die.'

The view of the Religious whose sexual energy is expended mainly in altruism seems to hide a dualism. Sexuality with its imperative, represents something which is irrational, or basic, and animal. This altruism may represent the hatred and fear of what is represented as primitive, and the fear of all passion. This seems to unearth the fear of death and loss of identity. St. Theda's heroism in her virginity was to avoid the fate that is worse than death: the annihilation of identity (Brown, 1990: 158). Perhaps that dualism can also be heard in the use of the word 'will', by its allocation instead of desire and its sexual connotation: 'Your lapse was a moment of weakness.' If weakness is viewed as the polarity of strength and will is of the mind, dualism is again revealed. The act of crisis is always viewed in the dualism as a negative experience and cannot be seen as a positive construct or one containing paradox. It cannot be viewed as being imbued with positive qualities, and marking a new stage of development. It cannot be understood in terms of meaning or ascesis.

'We do not have feelings,' as spoken, seems to be another aspect of the dualism of psyche and soma. Though a duality might be expressed as body and spirit, the same can be also be expressed as psyche and soma which is also endopsychic. What is the relationship of sensuality and sexuality? What is the understanding of the development of affect beyond instinct and drive theory? What is the source of this inhibition of feelings with reference to drives and instincts and ego development and ego synthesis? Is it an expression of the stoical, or the passionless, or is it the cry of the pre-Oedipal? All these suggested configurations of the selfless are possible. Do the Religious still have the capacity to fall in love if they say they have no feelings? (Thomas, 1986: 150). How does this affect maturation?

Benedicta Ward SLG, in an excellent study of repentance in early monastic sources and which she dedicated to Maria, a London prostitute, provides a negative view. She says:

> What concerned the monks of the early church was only one question, 'how can I be saved?' The literary tradition from that world shows them discovering the meaning of I in that question by a genuine awareness of the force of passion within themselves. Only when they had become aware of the force of this disintegration within themselves could they receive the gift of salvation which is Christ (1987: 104).

Such a negative view seems to present passion as fearful and chaotic. Passion in this view represents the fear of the annihilation of a person's identity. Are we only left with feelings when passion which is so much part of the construct of personality is denied? (Unger, 1984).

> 'A nun I once met said that she would not dream of kissing a sister who had come home after a long time on a foreign mission, because, we don't want to be effusive' (Moorhouse 1986: 198).

The sublimation of sexuality into work and altruism is a means to an end part of a global perspective. Yet it does not provide clarity as to whether the intention is one of love or hate.

Object relating can be a confusing exercise. Some people spend their lives in loving their object choice and others bind themselves in hate even to destroy the same or themselves. The choice of an object may represent a considerable ambivalence (Bergmann, 1971).

What is a passive sexuality? It is the conjecture of some people that Religious are able to live their lifestyle because they have a passive sexuality. It is a conjecture which allows no recognition that everybody's sexuality is different and varied. It also places the religious in another category from those of the world, namely as those not of the world. Those belonging to 'this world' according to this view, are subject to sexuality and passion. This categorisation belongs to the hierarchical and elitist view espoused by both Ambrose and Augustine after the collapse of the Roman Empire which made the celibate life with its unbroken and intact boundaries an ideal and the epitome of Christian life. His or her virginity was a sacred space prised loose from the world of biology and its causality (Brown, 1990: 432). The hierarchical view was at the expense of a perspective of community. Augustine's hierarchical view derivative of contemporary Roman culture can be compared with the earlier writings of the Shepherd of Hermas (Lightfoot, 1891, 1907). In the latter writing the virginity belonged to the whole community and not to an elite (Brown, 1990). The Augustinian view equated sexuality and death with both representing the loss of the primal harmony of body and soul. This view is also constructed upon the dualism of the rational and the irrational.

Are not holiness and sexuality compatible? Is this dualism also the mark and exercise of repression? Is it a sexuality which has no feelings because it contains a fear of identifying with the feminine (Thomas 1986). If this view equates feelings with 'the female', it is discriminatory towards women; degrading them and considering them to be inferior. Bailey (1954) also views the persecution of homosexuals in these terms. The ebb and flow of sexual energy is a crucial function between body and soul. It represents the ego and self in axis where it provides an answer to the question, 'How can I be my own friend and my own enemy?' (Brown, 1990: 239).

The sublimation of sexuality, as transposed into spiritual language, such as the image of the 'Bride of Christ' provides insight into the understanding of vocation. It is a nuptial model. This model's understanding of celibate sexuality is as an end in itself. The Child of Wisdom is another mystical image which provides an end in itself, in play (Greeley, 1975, 1984: 215).

Both are expressions of vocation. Distinctions can be made in terms of these categories. From these examples we can see vocation imagined as an end in itself but there is another category, and this sees vocation as means to a global vision or ministry.

Another conventional viewpoint would seem to arise out of envy and cynicism. A homosexual viewing the 'homosexual' nature of the Religious Life may see it as a haven which he or she does not have. The 'homosexuality' of the Religious Life exists within its structuring and in its being, as single sex communities (Moorhouse, 1969). For this observer viewing the haven it might be a place where homosexuals could live their lives undisturbed without persecution and hidden. With a wink they perceive it as a place of covert sexuality for they make the assumption that the community's members are free from restriction in a way that they are not. The restrictive rules of a community prevent that romantic and envious notion occurring. The notion of the wrongness of particular friendships has been used to mask to muffle and stifle homosexuality as well.

> What for example is the monk to do if he wakes up in the middle of the night bursting with sexual desire? Is he to masturbate? Is he to fling himself on the stone cold floor (as the handiest alternative to St. Benedict's nettle beds) in the hope that this will cool his ardour? Or is he merely to seize his breviary and trust that prayer will drive the demon out? A superior, far less inhibited than most, says that every one of these methods has been tried though very few people in religion are prepared to admit the existence of the first-or even of a situation which may require it (Moorhouse, 1969: 260).

This question remains as valid today, as it did in 1969. It is perhaps more valid now that homosexuality has come out of the closet in lay circles.

Chapter Four
Love and sexuality in psychoanalysis

Bergmann places love centrally in life and the human condition:

> In loving *and* being loved, lovers give each other a sense of uniqueness which only very few can find in other spheres of life (1980: 74).

N. O. Brown places it at the core of our humanity:

> The fundamental quest of man is to find an object for his love (1959, 1970: 7).

and Den Haag recognises its transcendence:

> In its highest sense love is a reaching for divine perfection, an act of creation. And it is always a longing (1964: 198).

There are differing concepts of love, and they are recognised by a choice of name, 'Agape, Amor, Eros, Libido' (Ireland, 1988: 15). Libido as one of these has its own contribution to make to the understanding of love within the continuing dialogue of ego and object in love and sexuality. Psychoanalysis recognises that the principal threats to our sexuality occur in relationships with others and especially those who are our significant others. This was recognised by Freud and manifested in the willingness to persevere with his early development of theory and clinical practice to provide an understanding of transference love. He found a basis for the neurosis in infantile sexuality. Freud's assertion from primary narcissism is that if we do not love we fall ill. Thus making the quest for love an imperative for any provision of health and wellbeing.

Transference love and mature love are similar but they have crucial differences. The transferences of psychoanalytical experience develop regardless of personality or appearance and can even disregard the sexuality and gender of the analyst or therapist. Those patients or clients who can idealise are able to establish a positive transference (Bergmann, 1980: 27).

Silverman (1988: 188) has mapped a passage of love for the patient or client from the infantile and the unrequited, through the erotic within the transference, and then returning back to love in real life.

An object relations theory would see the relationship of mature love as an enduring relationship maintained during the period of sexual maturity with an object of choice.

Bergmann's work has portrayed Sigmund Freud's development in this area but he also contends that after the 1920s Freud made no more significant contributions to a theory of love. It was in this period though that we see Freud titling some of his work as contributing towards a psychology of love (1910, 1912, 1918). Using this benchmark of the 1920s, Bergmann asserts that Freud's thinking was defined by his own theoretical development of mind. Bergmann is making reference to the topographical model in relation to the structural model. According to Freud's libidinal theory, after the earliest pregenital phases there is a split between tenderness and sensuality. Sensuality is first experienced in the oral and anal phases and then is submerged to arise at puberty at the stage of genital primacy where it re-joins tenderness. This is object relations constructed upon drive theory.

At any phase of development there is an overflow of libido, induced by frustration or inhibition. Libidinal desire can never be adequately satisfied as its original object was the mother. Its surfeit is sentient or sublimated. This is the ground for affection and tenderness and the development of love and other cultural pursuits. Freud's development of the structural model comes later. It is Bergmann's contention thus, that Freud never developed a coherent theory of love.

There are two aspects of love which assist the construction of theoretical development; loving as intrapsychic, and love of oneself and love of another, which is interpersonal and reflexive. This is expressed in libidinal theory by the separation of object choice into narcissistic and anaclitic object choice. The first is the choice of an object which is a reflection of the person's own narcissism and the other is an economic choice made which reflects an earlier or current dependency. Both represent the continual quest to know self and the other and to know sameness and to know difference in the same process. Excess in either the anaclitic or narcissistic can lead to psychic impoverishment by his or her bondage to an object or the exhaustion of libido. Bergmann sustains his own theorising by separating the state of falling in love, from the capacity to sustain love. I will follow the same line of thought even though at times the categorisation may seem contrived.

Libidinal theory, constructed firstly upon the topographic model and then the structural model argues that those who have mature object relations can love. It was Abrahams who, theorising after Freud, dominated this area until World War Two. The concept appears as a seemingly self-evident equation of genitality, post-ambivalent attitude and hence love. Otto Kernberg shares the same equation though his interpretation is beyond this being 'just orgasmic' and is more expansive, with a concern to distinguish that which needs to be integrated for mature object relations to occur (Bergmann, 1980). Bergmann disagrees with Kernberg that falling in love and staying in love are synonymous. Kernberg continues to make a contribution to this study of love in psychoanalysis (Ireland, 1988; Schlachet & Waxenberg, 1988 and others in Lassky & Silverman, 1988). Love in Abraham's theorising becomes synthesised under the supremacy of the genital phase and self-love or narcissism becomes an antagonistic force to object love. This theorising does not make a distinction between primary and secondary narcissism. Libidinal theory subsumes love as derivative of sexuality. After 1920 (*Beyond the Pleasure Principle*) Freud separated his use of Eros and libido. Libido became the more sexualised aspects of Eros.

The notion that libidinal choices are antagonistic and in a dualism is disputed by N. O. Brown who argues that this represents a confusion of categories (1959, 1970). He asserts that the goal of normal human adult love is union with the world in love and pleasure. This normal adult loving is the restitution of the primal condition of the original dyad of mother and infant. Brown's argument is based upon the crucible of primal love of mother and infant, which he identifies in Freud's writings. It is noteworthy that Rizutto also returns to this point for her own argument, describing it as the primary axis. Using libidinal theory, Brown asserts that the expression of love was not possessive but instead the desire for union.

It is also the time when the differentiation was made between the anaclitic object choice with its self-preserving and economic view, and the narcissistic with its object choice that mirrored its own self in argument derived from the primal situation union is an act of incorporation by the introjection of these object choices. This is transferable to the adult situation. The distinction between narcissistic or ego libido and object libido is lost. The essence of this argument is that the needs of the child to be loved is expressed in the love of the mother by the child. The love of the mother is thus essentially narcissistic.

The incorporation of lost objects in melancholia and mourning presents further opportunity for Brown's argument about the subject's relation to object; this time in loss. He further stresses the relationship between subject and object and the processes of identification which is fundamental to object choice. He makes the distinction between active identification and passive remodelling. Human libido for Brown is essentially narcissistic for it seeks a world to love as it loves itself with an aim to find itself in union with the world in love and peace.

Abraham's work enshrined the genital primacy in a heterosexual paradigm. It became a statement of normalcy which has been questioned, by those who have expanded the Oedipus myth, seeing homosexuality as part of the narrative (Kerenyi, 1991). Others building upon the Freudian notion of bisexuality have taken the view that the other object choice is just an alternative choosing and this questions a heterosexual normalcy with its view of a suppressed homosexuality (Jacobson, 1965). Some, with a view to the validity of earlier developmental stages having a psychosocial character, have underplayed its importance (Erikson, 1959, 1980).

Abraham's view took into account, the Oedipal Complex, with its new object choice, and its statements about gender and identity; the castration complex, with its agenda of development of individuation, and separation; and the overcoming of the incest taboo, which permitted sexual relationship with the new object. Abraham's work was a statement of a development from narcissism to object love, containing pre-ambivalent, ambivalent and post-ambivalent stages.

This libidinal development, I believe, requires further perspective. It seems one-sided. Compare Loewalds' statement; 'Love as a force or power-brings people together – but also brings oneself together – into one individuality which we become by identification' (1978: 40). His reflexive view of the relationship, with its mutuality and integration in love and continuing dialectic, seem also to be part of the reflections of the structural model of personality and ego psychology. The intentionality of subject and object is more pronounced. It still asserts that sexuality is the primary expression of love and the focus of feelings of love.

Libidinal theory allows for developmental phases at an intrapsychic level. It is still mainly concerned with the psychology and psychopathology of sexuality that interfere with the capacity to love, rather than the various states of loving. I continue with Bergmann's (1980) distinction between falling in love, and being in love. The distinction implies that there are appropriate developmental tasks to be completed. 'Falling in love' in Freud's terms and developed through the 'Three Essays' (1905) and 'The Three Caskets' (1913), is 'the finding of the object, which is a re-finding of the object' (Freud, 1905: 222). It places infant sexuality and the primary caregiving experience at the core of the experience of falling in love.

Bergmann (1971), continuing to utilise Margaret Mahler's work, believes that the longing of the falling in love is a recalling of the original symbiotic relationship of mother and baby and the desire for that experience again. His construct is not based upon the primary narcissism but in the mother-infant matrix.

Projection, in the search for a sexual object, develops from the presence of an ego ideal and the wishful concepts of oneself. This projection is the seeking of the sexual ideal.

Bergmann (1980) further develops this to include the ability to test the reality and evaluate the possibility of a long-term relationship (Freud, 1910). The projection is dependent upon the condensation of earlier introjects as signified in the topographic model or by the unconscious ego in the structural model. In Freud's (1915) 'Instincts and Vicissitudes', he postulates the three opposites; of loving and hating, to loving-indifference, loving and being loved. This expresses less of the instinct and drive theory, but more of an entire self or subject, relating to the object. It seems to show the direction of Freud's development of thought.

There are, according to Bergmann (1980), additional functions for the ego in 'falling in love'. There are, for him or her, conflicts to be overcome between the ego and the superego with regard to the overcoming of the incest taboo, and between the ego and the id to counteract what are considered impossible demands. There is also the task to get the new subject to conform to the original subject. The hope exists also that there can be restitution for experiences of the pre-Oedipal phase. The hope is that any childhood experience may be altered in the new. To be able to fall in love is a significant task and it seems to indicate affective maturing for a person. Love becomes the process by which Oedipal and incestuous ties might be resolved.

When there is a move from 'falling in love' to 'staying in love' there is a move into the arena of ego psychology. Psychoanalysis begins to contend a higher integration of the instincts in ego psychology and the development of affect. Waelder (1930) and Michael Balint (1947) are cited by Bergmann as significant in creating building blocks in this theoretical development. I have already raised the question of the relation of mature objects to sexuality but ego psychology which is the fruit of Freud's structural model takes this further. Its significance is in determining the choice of object through ego ideal and reality testing. The person has to be able to endure those affects which are distressing and hateful (for example envy and aggression) with sufficient love, whilst sustaining his or her individuality in 'the staying in love'.

For the attachment to a few persons classical theory presupposes an aim inhibited libidinal development. It presupposes that this also is the basis for intimacy and caring for each other in a mutually acceptable manner whilst allowing for competitiveness as part of that intimacy. It involves the move from an idealisation to the recognition of the reality of the actual person(s). The areas of narcissism, dependency and loss are crucial areas to be experienced and endured, as they prepare for object choice and staying in love. The pubertal integration preceding object choice covers the area of passive and sexual excitement, and tenderness and caring. It recalls Freud's division of instinct in prepubertal libidinal theory. For Balint, the engagement in the prolonged emotional tie was a re-finding of the devotion of parent and child. He constructed his theorising on a primary love. In the longing for what was lost, Bergmann found expression of the prolonged emotional tie of Margaret Mahler's symbiotic relationship of mother and child. In a reflection of Winnicott, Bergmann notes, 'Those who cannot love. cannot be alone with the love object. They need entertainment. and socialisation and prefer short sexual encounters. Object constancy and the capacity to love is not always appreciated' (Bergmann 1971: 33).

Love in the Kleinian developmental framework of Object Relations, which moves from the paranoid schizoid to the depressive positions, is the discovery of love through sexuality. It is love arising out of guilt and reparation in a cyclical basis. Libidinal theory (Freudian) subsumes love as derivative of sexuality. In the depressive position of the Kleinian framework, integration and the toleration of ambivalence are the paramount features. Although Object Relations begins in the sphere of primary love and as all life from its perspective is object relations, it provides a different framework. It is also a reminder that in the classical position there are age-appropriate stages of development and that love is considered to be a higher integration.

The 'wish of wish fulfilment' (Owen, 1993. 229) lies at the heart of classical theorising. It promotes the notion of desire and the search for meaning. Longing is an essential part of integration and the desire for another. Longing contains a measure of altruism and an understanding of need. It leaves us alone in a solitude, without gratification. 'It causes us to face death, and to be connected with people and rooted in human experience' (Davis, 1988: 171). Longing stands between desire and fulfilment, and gratification alters it (Den Haag, 1964).

> To feel the I and the You the fear that life may run out before such feeling has been experienced in love. No other affliction makes it equally clear that ego psychology alone cannot encompass central human problems which so far have been left to poetry or metaphysics (Erikson, 1968, 1983: 217).

The integration of 'what' qualities provides us with the sexual object? We can list genital arousal, and excitement, the capacity for orgasmic pleasure with feelings of tenderness and caring for the other. Yet as Altman (1977) says for staying in love, we require the duration of identity alongside the ability to endure frustration. Bellak (1970) in a light-hearted manner makes reference to an intimacy index, as though it were two porcupines huddling together on a wintry day for warmth; too close meant pain from the quills and too far apart meant there was insufficient warmth.

Wisdom speaks of the paradox of love, which creates the

exchanges of selves in this maturity. His construct is a development from the Hegelian dialectic:

> Where objects seek to transform one another, and then surrender to one another. In the dialectic of subject and object, the subject (1) creates the object, (2) dominates and remodels it, (3) is dominated and remodelled by it, (4) absorbs it. (5) loses itself in it, and finally (6) fuses absolutely with it while retaining its own identity (1970: 349).

There are the elements of self-interest and its contrary, self-demotion, and the 'highly personal'. The latter is a response to a social image of relationship. He draws out the qualities of attractiveness, high valuation of one another, love, selflessness and self-demotion which provide the basis for mutual understanding. Mutual understanding in this exchange provides the ground for shared feelings in contrast to sympathy. It is the characteristic which has much in common with empathy. His second characteristic is the shared experiences which he describes as transactional experiences and 'personality mingling'. Finally there is the ground for growth in terms of what a person may become.

The capacity for the loving relationship may offer other areas of fulfilment. Forms of attachment may change so that larger realms of involvement might be encompassed. This allows for the alteration of ego ideals where those already posited are replaced by others, and new identifications can be made. There is the transcending of the self as well, as in the participation in the transformation of another. This is a reminder of the transpersonal in a matrix. In the fusion of self in this oscillation, occasions for the loss of self are to be compared with the possibilities for the consolidation and the emergence of new aspects of the self

Love is subsumed by sexuality in psychoanalysis. Psychoanalysis is marked by its characteristics of abstinence and neutrality. Whether we speak of 'falling in love', or 'staying in love' in a libidinal theory, this is contingent upon the value system we employ. The relationship between nature and culture is at the heart of psychoanalytical theory.

> As a psychological rule, this is surely wrong: it can be as healthy to frustrate as it is to gratify one's desires. Sometimes gratification is very unhealthy; sometimes frustration is. Nor can psychological health be accepted as morally decisive. If we do, it makes no sense to call a rule unnatural merely because it restrains an urge; the urge is no more natural than any other. The combination of love and sex is no more natural than separation. Thus what we decide about restraining, or indulging an emotion or a sexual urge, rests on religious, social or personal values, none of which can claim to be more natural than the other (Den Haag. 1964: 199).

Chapter Five
The image of the heart and the heart's desire

> But Marx, lacking the concept of repression and the unconscious-that is to say, not being prepared to recognize the mystery of the human heart-could not pursue the line of thought implied in his own epigram. Psychoanalysis is equipped to study the mystery of the human heart, and must recognize religion to be the heart of the mystery. But psychoanalysis can go beyond religion only if it sees itself as completing what religion tries to do, namely, make the unconscious conscious; then psychoanalysis would be the science of original sin. Psychoanalysis is in a position to define the error in religion only after it has recognized the truth (Brown, 1959, 1970: 13).

Norman Brown draws together the heart in the context of psychoanalytical thought and in religion and places it centrally for us. The unconscious is the source of wish and desire.

The heart has become the focus for identification of affect, and identifiable as its source. We perceive it as the seat of emotions. This imaging separates it from the original organ of the physical body. In a Judaeo-Christian anthropology which has its basis in Christian scripture, the heart is the centre of the person. This involves us psychologically in two ways. There is the centrality of the focussing, and the personal, which is constituted by the imaginal 'I' and a cognitive/affective awareness which acknowledges a self. The physical organ called the heart has become part of a descriptive and symbolic language and is also identified with a place of loving and a place of desiring. In relationships it becomes the place in this imaginative exercise, where the person is most aware of him or herself, as another body and his or herself, as the subject or object in relation to others.

Within intrapersonal dimensions, the heart is also in regard and having a relationship to the other parts of the body and the economy of a person's anatomy. In different cultures the organs have different attributes. The kidneys or the liver in particular, may signify different affects. Elkin's study of Australian Aboriginal medicine men makes reference to the caul or the fat of the kidneys. In that Australian context it is also important for 'the making of medicine men'. The fear also exists that in the medicine man's sorcery, the taking of kidney fat would injure a person's spirit (Elkin, 1977). Peter Brown makes reference to the kidneys as representing the source of sexuality. Monastic thought in the early Christian period considered them to be the place where the shadows lingered longer (Brown, 1988, 1990). They were 'the inmost parts'. Though this may vary from culture to culture, it provides a narrative and a meaning for the essential interpretation, to one self and to others, about both the body and the person. Because the person is expressive of context, we can by inference encompass both community and all human society and societies. Similarly I consider the Freudian narrative of psychosexual development to be marked by descriptions of oral, anal, phallic, latent and genital stages. This too, is descriptive of the body and also contains a hierarchy of development which is psycho-biological. The Freudian narrative argues its validity and accuracy in terms of scientific investigation through the basis of clinical work.

Freudian psychology at its beginning noted the power of transference when it stumbled upon the vital ingredients in combination, of both love and imagination. Josef Breuer stumbled as some of his patients fell in love with him while it was Sigmund Freud who in persevering, was able to comprehend this phenomenon. Freud's utilising of this phenomenon enabled him to provide the basis for a theoretical understanding of psychic conflict and repression. He opened up the area of its subjectivity. Although psychoanalysis does not seem to allow for a philosophy of the heart (Hillman, 1992), its psychosexual development did find expression in culture. It was able to theoretically place the wish at the centre of its edifice rather than the thought.

My attention is also drawn to Winnicott's work at this juncture. He placed need at the centre of his edifice and as prior to a person's discovery of desire in frustration. He felt that desire belonged to a more sophisticated level of development. 'The mutuality' of mother and infant was a place where instinctual drives were not specifically involved. He concentrated upon this 'world' of the communication of anatomy and physiology of bodies, where the illusion was created and a unity without a distinction between the internal or external existed

(Winnicott, 1989). Object relatedness occurs at a different level of integration and at a different age in this construct.

Jacobson's expression of her work deals with self-representations and imagination. I believe these to be essential for endopsychic imagery.

> 'They' refer to the ambiguous use of the term ego; i.e. to the lack of distinction between the ego which represents a structural mental system, the self, which I defined above and the self-representations … Hartman (1950) called attention to this point [and] suggested the use of the latter term (analogous to object representativeness) for the unconscious, preconscious and conscious endopsychic representations of the bodily and mental self in the system ego. I have worked with this concept for years, because I have found it indispensable for investigation of psychotic disorder (Jacobson, 1965: 18).

When we fall in love we begin to imagine and when we imagine we then fall in love (Hillman, 1992). Hence the heart which engages in a dialogue must imagine.

A narrative which includes the heart and its desires provides a basis for dialogue and communication about affects, which develop as when a self and an other are recognisable. They are embodied. The multiplicity of instincts, their integration, and ego development are linked. There is a hierarchy of development in so much as the complexity of integration increases according to age and maturing. What is possible for a baby is different for a child of three or four years old. Love and hate are significant for the understanding of maturation, in that they are object and ego related. Mood as a different word, is more diffuse and shows less concern for object relatedness (Jacobson, 1971).

Yet heart can mean many different things. I think James Hillman's description of the human heart as being threefold and developmental is a presentation which helps unfold this. He says we should think firstly of the heart as being of our humanity

> First: my heart is my humanity, my courage to live. my strength and my fierce passion. By means of it nothing is foreign to me. My most noble virtues emanate from the heart: loyalty, heroic boldness, compassion. Let us call this the heart of the lion, Coeur de Lion. Second: my heart is an organ of the body. It is a muscle or a pump. an intricate mechanism and secret holder of my death. Let us refer to this pumping heart as the heart of Harvey. Third: my heart is my love, my feelings, the locus of my soul and sense of person. It is the place of intimate interiority. where sin, and shame and desire, and the unfathomable divine inhabit. Let us call this personal heart, the heart of Augustine (Hillman, 1992: 9).

We can have all three of Hillman's hearts.

We are often confronted by Augustine of Hippo's words when talking of a Christian's relationship to God or the Divine:

> For thou hast stirred him up that he may take pleasure in praising thee; because thou has created us for thyself, and our hearts know no rest, until it may repose in thee. Grant then, 0 God, that I may know and understand whether of these two things be first to call upon thee or to praise thee, and whether it be first to know thee or to call upon thee? (St. Augustine, 1960: 7).

It does not clarify the notion of the heart but does place it as central in the life of the Christian and their concept of faith, and by implication makes it a central feature of the Divine and a place of the soul. The quote from the first chapter which has at its subheading 'He is kindled with the desire of praising God.' Already we are talking of its centrality. And that centrality is at the centrality of person and the experience of self.

It seems also to be held in balance and counterpoise by the dichotomy of mind and heart which also reflects the relationship of body and soul. The imaging of our self is also the imaging of a body or bodies. It is central to a body–mind relationship or in the language of Winnicott, 'psyche and soma'. Mind is only one aspect of psyche and soma and any consideration about mind is also a consideration about mind as a feature of the psyche and soma relationship. Rizutto provides Laplanche and Pontalis' explanation of the relationship of psyche and soma, 'The relation between soma and psyche is conceived of as neither parallelistic or causal; rather it is to be understood by the analogy with the relationship between a delegate and his mandator' (1979: 61).

Cartesian thought has directed us away from a contemplative worldview. The contemplative perspective is an alternative to a compassionate world view. Both contemplation and compassion are the expressions of a universal view. with both containing a dialogue between the individual and his or her community and the heart. The overview may not simply be that the heart is the place of feeling and the mind the source and place of thought and mental activity. James Hillman argues that the heart is capable of thought. 'Our hearts cannot apprehend that they are imaginatively thinking hearts, because we have been so long told that the mind thinks and the heart feels and that imagination leads us astray from both' (1992: 6).

Heart and mind are symbolic as they are part of the act of imagination which in any given situation helps us understand 'I'. This is the 'I' which seems to be guarded by integrity and which is monosyllabic. Similarly the self might be experienced through subjectivity as feelings or it might be conceived as being thoughts and concepts (Liddon, 1989).

The Christian anthropology communicating in a symbolic language, notes that heart and love are in some way linked together. Love as a word and a subject apart from the act of falling-in-love, includes other words such as lust, desire, passion which are related to other objects or subjects. It seems reflexive and enables a better perception and evaluation of self. Love is to be held and understood in relationship. *The Interpreter's Dictionary of the Bible* traverses the Christian Scriptures revealing their plurality. From the commentary on the Pauline Letter to the Ephesians in chapter one verse eighteen: 'The intellect is not the centre of our real selves. For that citadel of the soul which stands guard over love, hate, loyalty and treachery, trust and mistrust, we still have no better word than the heart' (Buttrick et al, 1979. Vol.10: 629).

And using commentary from other books of the scriptures within the same volumes and with regard to their exegesis, we are informed that the heart was not the seat of the emotions but the seat of the intellect (Vol. 8: 126). The kidneys symbolise the seat of the emotions (Psalm 139: 13); also 'the heart is regarded as the seat of consciousness and the will' (Vol. 4: 811), even more specifically, 'it figures most prominently as the instrument of man's intellectual and volitional activity' (Vol. 4: 793). It also seems to concur with purity of vision and a capacity for insight (Vol. 7: 285a).

This is scant information from which to embark upon the notion of a Christian anthropology as contained in the writings of Christian scripture. Although brief it does recognise the context of Semitic thought. It informs us that the heart is not only the seat of emotions, although more specifically this was located in the organs of the kidneys but that it also contained cognition. With due regard to the various cosmologies and contexts this does present a picture of the heart in a different way from a dichotomy of heart and mind which in simplistic terms might be thought of solely as feeling and thought. If there is a language which deals with emotions, and desire and will, which seems to step outside of present theoretical constructs, and is not a presentation of fantasy but of reality and is more than a matrix of the mind; then the conjunction of heart and mind requires a different exposition.

H. Richard Niebuhr (McDargh, 1983: 104), when discussing

how an individual comes to faith, links the process of faith with 'the reasoning of the heart':

> That activity whereby the human person makes personal sense of the cumulative weight of the past, the total impinging reality of the present moment, and the lure or terror of the future. The reasoning of the heart is not the objective, discursive and dispassionate operation of the mind, though it is a cognitive operation and by no means anti-rational. It is the affective act of interpretation of our total experience. Its medium is not abstract concepts that can be coolly and critically manipulated. Its material is images, the living products of the human imagination, Niebuhr sadly recognizes that we know this reasoning of faith more often in its broken form in which it involves the evil imaginations of the heart, the distorted images of self and others that is at the root of our mistrust and fearfulness and envy before the prospect of community (Niebuhr, 1941: 71-100).

Within the language of psychoanalysis this reflection is comparable to the quest for reality which grows in self knowledge

This reflection of Niebuhr's at the place where psychology and theology meet, contains the same enthusiasm for a philosophy of the heart which Hillman recognises in the work of the Sufi scholar Corbin. It also takes us into dimensions of madness and of sanity giving recognition to those times and places when the psychic structure is overflowing with emotion. Heart and mind in conjunction are then dysfunctional and passion is consuming and even poisonous. This is expressed well by Unger (1984). I feel that I am trying to place within familiar and normative theoretical constructs the hypothesis of new argument.

Unger's work in terms of personality *Passion: An Essay on Personality,* seems far from psychoanalytical language, yet provides further insight into the heart. He defines passion as being of emotions and affects and more (1984: 287). To write about emotions and affect in terms of drive theory in the way that Jacobson and Glover do; although Brierley pauses to make a leap (Rayner, 1990), seems to not pass a divide which Guntrip identifies as having been first made by Freud in 1926 in his theory of anxiety. Guntrip (1977) identified that a new development in ego-psychology was in process, that of liberating psychoanalysis from an excessive psycho-biological bias and providing a reorientation towards a psychological theory of personality.

Unger's contributions in his appendix entitled 'A Program for Late Twentieth Century Psychiatry' (1984) places his discussion about the personality within the mind and body dichotomy. I think this is important for my consideration of the heart. Unger (1984: 281) says:

> The organic facts are mediated and redirected by a personal drama … the study of the biochemical triggers, residues and counterparts of mental disease is no substitute for the analysis of the internal world

> of the imagination and, above all, of the imagination of the selfhood and relationship, whose crisis constitutes the heart of the psychotic event.

I have already given some airing to a notion of narrative.

The personal drama will undoubtedly incorporate objects in relation to the self and these may be objects of choice and even desire. It is at this point that I find Unger's words particularly helpful. I also incorporate the Oedipal Complex at this point which contains both narrative and psychoanalytical concepts and I return to the point that the maturity of object choice is essential for genital primacy or sexual maturity. A distinction can be made between psychological acting-out which is considered pathological, and the nature of the psyche with its complexes which are directive of development. These are two different situations but both highlight the mind and body relationship.

In Dollimore's (1991) work, *Sexual Dissidence,* we see the homosexual who extends him or herself into 'camp'. In Freud's study of Dora (Rose, 1991) we see a woman who identifies herself with another. These in their different contexts exhibit the power of the imagination to identify with another and to reorient or rediscover themselves. This is the power of transference though we embark now on the capacity of the person to disidentify and to understand the meaning for himself or herself. I return to Brown's distinction between active identification and passive remodelling. The discussion returns to the self or the enduring identity. Yet cast in the ground of mind and body relationships it enlivens as it reflects the statements of Ferenczi, that there will be no development in psychotherapeutic work unless there is expression of emotion and affect. Unger reflects that:

> The experience of passion is located at the point where distinctions between desire (wanting something from the other person) and knowledge (viewing himself and ourself in a certain way) collapse. Together with collective experiments in the organisation of work, it is the substratum from which more articulate images of society are drawn. It is the liquid form into which these images melt back at times of heightened practical or visionary strife (Unger, 1984: 287).

Surely what might be said of the society can also be said of the individual.

Unger (1984) embraces, faith, hope and love as transforming emotions: transforming realities where even love and hate can be cyclical and destructive and transforming because they have the force and element of surprise. We are more ready to see the destructiveness of hate and need to be reminded in Thomas Traherne's (1927: 121) words of loving right: 'Never was anything in this world loved too much. but many things in a false way; and all in too short a measure.' And to recall Unger's expression of this concern with love and hate and transforming realities:

> 'We may be unable to tell whether a dominant picture of personal or social reality gives better insight into

> the facts and possibilities of a historical situation than the emotions that disrupt this picture' (1984: x).

McDargh is inclined to call 'faith, hope and love 'metaphysical' and to argue that through beliefs affect is expressed in consensual terms and credal statements. For McDargh the metaphysical precedes the scientific:

> 'What I am suggesting is that at a level of development prior to conceptual expression, and in many ways prior even to consciousness. for every human being "metaphysics" precedes psychics' (McDargh, 1983: 80).

The use of the word metaphysical is not so compatible as might be first thought with psychoanalytical language. In a doctrine of religious experience revelation comes as gift and because it is given without prior consideration of merit or worthiness, it is deemed an act of love and received as love in love. It is comparable in this way to the original matrix of mother and baby. This anthropomorphism is I believe valid as are all images of the experience of the divine which are perceived through the original object relations. These images may be negative or positive and the realisation of these three affects, of faith, hope and love may be the fruit of psychotherapeutic work with regard to the original object relationships which were the ground of the imaging. This imaging also encompasses the recognition of self-representation in the subject's being related to other objects. On this occasion the object is the Divine.

This can be extended to reflect upon the relationship of

language and feelings and as to show how these come to be expressed in terms of consensual agreement of tradition as expressions of the faith and doctrine of communities (even Institutes of Psychoanalysis).

This 'metaphysics' is something which also appears in Elkin's reference (1977: 170) to Dr. J.E. Cawte who recorded in his 1974 book *Medicine is the Law,* the observation that the 'Aboriginal Men of High Degree' mobilised 'faith and hope' as healing emotions in the same way that psychotherapeutic practitioners did elsewhere. It is an obscure reference but as it transcends cultures it is enlightening.

The ideal of 'the child' represents a move away from rationalist thinking. As a religious ideal the innocence of childhood has resisted assimilation into a rational theological tradition.

N. O. Brown asserts that Freud in his articulation of the doctrine of infantile sexuality makes a scientific reformulation and reaffirmation of the religious and poetical theme of the innocence of childhood. Rather than it being seen as a 'return' to an innocence it becomes the preferred and indestructible goal of life:

> 'Then what is the pattern of activity, free from human work, the serious business of life, and the reality principle, which is adumbrated in the life of children? The answer is that children play' (Brown, 1970: 32).

It is the activity which unites us with the objects of our love. If the words of Freud have significance, that our maturity and adulthood is to love and work, then this makes sense. If the erotic is the ultimate essence of our being then activity is according to the pleasure principle. This innocence, which is deemed to be of the heart as well as of the mind, is a link with the ideal of the child and with heart. It is affirmed in the mystics and heretics, such as Francis of Assisi, Jacob Boehme; the poets, Blake and Rilke; Rousseau, and even Freud himself

Perhaps, as Brown (1970) comments, Freud is unable to see how this goal is reconcilable to the deep commitment which humanity has to culture and cultural progress. It is also a link between the poetic metaphor and the unconscious; where there is no higher and lower and no dualisms. The ideal and innocence and the heart are drawn together. James Hillman reflects on the childhoods recaptured by therapies; and asks us to remember that they are not only those of our childhood and of reduction but also Platonic and ideal childhoods. He describes them as: 'the a priori remembrance of imaginal presences transferred with us into this life and the source of its life' (1992: 9).

It is the concurrence of the confessional with a sense of presence and self-consciousness.

This is revealed in the medieval allegories of the Virgin and the Unicom. This allegory is favoured as a theme in Religious Life where Religious in the use of allegory explore their own existence as phenomena and as 'the beloved'. Thus they perceive their existence as 'subjects' and as 'beloved' and explore a love which is not only reflexive; but also seeing themselves as singular. In Caroline Glyn's stories *Dream and Vision* (1977), titled 'A Mountain at the End of Night' we find 'The Unicorn', and amongst other of her titles we find 'The Unicorn Girl'. In Gramick (1989: 78), Sister Raphaela writes in 'Home by Way of Roundabout': 'Celibacy for me was the skein by which the unicorn drew the maiden.'

These examples are part of a wider theme which is spelt out by Beer (1977). The conjunction of the virgin and the unicorn becomes an affect which is greater than the sum of its parts. It is part of a reality which does not come from logic but from the fable and story belonging to the European history of ideas (Beer, 1977).

La Dame a la Licorne is a series of six tapestries in the Musée de Thermes et l'Hôtel de Cluny in Paris. Five tapestries of the five senses are surmounted by a sixth entitled 'À Mon Seul Désir' where 'will' purifies the other senses and integrity is redeemed:

> 'À Mon Seul Désir' reveals the true meaning of the series. It should be considered as relating to the Liberum Arbitrium of the Greek philosophers who believed that freedom from the passions provoked by ill controlled senses would ensure right behaviour' (Erlande-Brandenburg,1989: 13).

Brandenburg translates its title as meaning, 'in accordance only with my will' (1989: 69). The cast-off necklace becomes the symbol of renunciation of the passions aroused and when they are not under control.

The Hunting of the Unicorn belongs to a similar collection of Medieval art in the Cloisters Museum in New York (Beer,

1977; Sipress,1974) where the theme is the hunt, and the capture of the unicorn is possible when lured by the virgin. Longing is the fruitful ground of the virgin. This longing is a longing without possession. It is the reflection of the volition of the heart in both will and desire. The Virgin remains ever virgin and fertile in desire. Themes of annunciation and conception become applicable, although in paradox, for will and desire become translated into object desire. This returns to my theme and the theme of this dissertation: the heart's desire. The wish of the person is to be a ground for discovering that choice and desire, repeatedly and in different contexts and through different selves.

The process of integration is by love. Anger and hate are needed also for processes of separation and for the establishment of autonomy through the toleration of ambivalence. The identification in the body of a place of integration is 'the heart' and whatever that means in its complexity. Love acts in a dialectic with hate. Although psychosomatic illness locates ill health in places and parts of the body and seems a less than articulate expression of mental pain and confusion, it is also a symbolisation. As a symbolisation it is reflexive, in that it involves other objects and subjects. It should not be necessarily regarded as primitive or archaic in character and should neither necessarily be perceived as being non-verbal or even pre-verbal. Juliet Mitchell argues that identification is the forerunner of symbolism and is the foundation of all sublimation and talent 'since it is by way of symbolic equation that things, activities and interest become the subject of libidinal phantasies' (1986: 97).

She has placed symbolisation within ego development. McDargh (1983), also regards it as being of a higher level of integration and argues for a better comprehension of the phenomena.

Edith Jacobson has written: 'The relation between denial and psychotic loss of object and self cathexis certainly requires thorough clinical and theoretical scrutiny' (1971: 135).

This presenting of the relationship between self and object and their interrelatedness makes symbolisation something more or different than a somatisation. In the standard edition of Sigmund Freud's work I found only two references to the word 'heart' They were in *The Interpretation of Dreams* (1901) on pages 86 and 225. It was the same reference to the heart which he introduced as the stuff of dreams where if pain was to be identified with a particular part of the body it was recognisable by symbol as the source of the stimulus: 'The heart will be represented by hollow boxes or baskets' (Freud 1900: 86).

Joyce McDougall (1989) in *Theaters of the Body* is more expansive. She wanted to present what she called the psychosomatic potentiality on the part of every individual. She was wrote about 'the heart' in two chapters, one entitled 'The Reasons of The Heart' and the other, 'The Grief That Has No Vent in Tears'. The second was the case study of Tim whose childhood ideal was she said, to be 'heartless':

> If poets, lovers and mystics have always known that 'the heart hath reasons that reason knoweth not,' it is perhaps because they intuitively sense that the heart is the essential organ of affect, the metaphor

> of love, grief, and nostalgia as well as of hatred, rage, and violence. The fragments of analysis that follows reconstructs the analytic story of a man whose childhood ideal was to be 'heartless', so that he might feel neither physical or mental pain (McDougall, 1989: 118).

I commenced this chapter with the sense that 'heart' was a thing or an object to which we could have relationship, even though it might also give sense to self through its centrality. And it seems we can do this in relation to our own bodies, in the same way that we can be object to other objects, and even though we can be subjects to ourselves. It was my intention to take the discussion of 'heart' away from being cast solely in terms which might be psychosomatic. The objects which we might be object to; might even be the faeces produced by our own body or a work which is created, an opus, or as the parts and organs of our body in relationship to each another. It is my concern to see the continued expression of the relationship of ourselves to objects and the loss which can cause the loss of a sense of self. This loss of relationship and loss of self is different from the psychosomatic displacement. The abnormal can lend itself to reflection of the normal.

Edith Jacobson (1977) believed that she was expanding Freud's thesis with the idea that psychotics may convert into object substitutes, not only words but any split-off, formal psychic elements. She queried how far this withdrawal of the cathexis from objects and from the self is induced by processes of denial of external and internal reality.

The metaphor continues as language of the body and the self. Helman can write thus:

> In this exchange, both donor and recipient quite literally lost their heart to one another, via the matchmakers of medical science, so that afterwards with his heart 'in the right place', a man who had been sick of heart could resume his everyday life. as 'hearty' as before (Helman 1991: 3).

A person's self-representation can thus be focussed even within the narrative of sickness and health. It may be unclear whether this imaginal language with its imagery and metaphor which can focus on the 'I' (Hillman, 1992), represents an ego-development (Jacobson, 1965). It is certainly addressing the self-representation in an aesthetic sense, which is the link between 'the heart' and the sense perceptions. Together 'the heart' and the senses contribute to a self-perception, in fragments and also in the development and the exploration of a unified sense of self or selves. To transpose the self for the ego would be a simplification. If we are to continue to reflect upon 'the heart's desire' that needs to be kept in mind.

A self-representation is fundamental, as fundamental as the development of a sense of 'I' and a sense of body in relation to the other; for a description of identity and an acknowledgement of person. The understanding of affects is necessary for an understanding of self, or for a language which pertains to them. This self-representation is apart from any biological manifestation although developed from drive theory, and yet essential as part of a self-consciousness. I believe the essence of this discussion as carried on in its many forms is the relation of the subject and the object. I propose the words of McDargh: 'The substance of this awareness is that there is an essential connection between self and object representations and the formation of self' (1983: 116).

The relation to the object is not the same in every circumstance, event and occasion. I have already made reference to objects of choice and objects of desire. I have made reference to objects as they are to the persons concerned. This also allows us to consider the transitional object as it occurs in Winnicott's language and which may or may not have a distinct identity. Whatever the reasons for choice whether as acts of defence or distinct from desire, it seems that they signal that 'love' is a developmental level where there can be intersubjectivity and relationship. Love may be symbiotic, mutually dependent or equally partnered. The recognition of love in this way draws also upon the words 'reality' and its contrast 'illusion', which although used in psychotic exploration is also the substance of definition in areas of religious experience.

Chapter six
Maturing in the religious life

The attainment of a solemn profession of vows appears as a sign of membership and the reward of perseverance. That is all that is necessary for belonging to a community and once this thread has been established all life is lived in relation to the vows, according to life's exigencies and circumstances. Then the vows can be reflected upon and the charism of the community can be reflected upon also. The vows have become the architect and achievement of recognition in the religious community. What more can be said? There has been a trial period and a testing: a noviciate. This experimentation has taken place and we now see a graduation ceremony. There appears to be an underlying assumption that all tasks have been done and from now experience will be gained by offices held in the community or externally through ministry. The work of faith is now constituted and the life of conversion commences.

There is another argument however, that human development goes on, and within that there are further developmental goals (Erikson, 1959, 1984). This requires recognition. The schema of development of maturity through the vows which I have outlined may be considered insufficient. There is a need for other goals and further life experiences. 'Holiness' is stated as a recognised goal but if there is an expectation of a human maturity which is deemed adult, what does 'holiness' mean? 'Love' is a word which is used as a goal also. Some would say, 'the capacity to love'. The latter is highlighted by the work of McDargh (1983), and the writings of Bergmann (1971). Freud said that we needed to love or we would fall ill. His concern was with narcissism which became a pivotal issue. This places love within the scope of health. Renunciation and sacrifice are words which are often utilised by Religious as demarcating holiness. 'Of this world' and 'not-of-this world' are also spoken of. The categorisation is constituted as though it can only be either a renunciation of worldly values and a desire for perfection in and through celibacy, or an avowal of the world and the natural order. McDargh views the development of faith and the development of self:

> To say that faith must be regarded developmentally is only to acknowledge that at every bend and turn in the course of life, the confluence of circumstance, social factors and the maturation and declination of one's personal capacities, faculties and talents presents a new claim on one's sense of self. It as though life says, 'Here, can you accommodate this piece of reality … Can you enlarge your map of the world (i.e. your map of yourself in the world) to include the fact of your sexuality the mystery and design of the sexuality of another person, this loss and that gain, the awareness of your own finitude, the intrusive face of your own death?' At the advent of each of these crises – these

> dangerous opportunities and opportune dangers – there is an assent that must be summoned from the depths of those psychic resources which constitute us as selves (1983: 88).

The affectional and the spiritual are often confused as intertwined and as if there was no difference between them. Their relationship is not understood. N. O. Brown said there was always need of an object to love. This can be compared to Fairbairn and to Klein where libido needs an object not just a cathexis. McDargh expresses a similar idea, within the notion that a subject requires love in return. It points to the realm of affect and its maturation not just as a priori to spiritual maturity, but in fact containing the desired holiness in the way that Schneiders' denotes it: 'the substrate'.

The celibate is a solitary whose sexuality is expressed through his or her celibacy. This seems the most difficult to comprehend. If there is to be love for a continued development and growth, the importance of human relationships and a variety of relationships is extremely important. Even a solitary person requires a defined and social context. He or she is no different from fellows in the world. Friendship beyond the environs of the religious community become important and the relationship of the individual and the communal are tested in the allowing of space, time and the importance of this. The Religious Life cannot articulate a division between love of God and love of humanity, as though the latter was secondary. The Christian scriptures argue that love of God is possible if love of humanity is known and understood. Thus is indicated in the

Christian tradition, that being able to love on a psychosexual level is the basis for a love relationship with God. This also requires loving the particular, before loving the universal.

'One of the most consistent characteristics of the great lovers of God and personally effective ministers in Church history is the capacity for deep personal relationships. and their actual friendships' (Schneiders. 1986: 220).

Loving an object requires the ability to tolerate dependency along with a tolerance of ambivalence and having a sense of one's own reality. These are the words of McDargh's (1983) schema. It requires the capacity to be alone, not just in loneliness but in the positive experience of solitude. Bergmann's (1971) comments are useful here, when reflecting on the experience of the person who cannot tolerate their own company, and as to how it leads him or her to short sexual encounters, and acting out and diversions. Loving an object belongs also to the notion that a person will be having a relationship to a real and meaningful world. The interception of meaning is extremely important, in its reflexiveness and in the relationship of the objects and their world. Reality is a learnt experience.

The person in relationship is a total person and yet of varying stages of integration and experience. In his or her relating, there is sexuality and eroticism as he or she relates to another or experiences another person. There cannot be a denial of it, or its repression, or there is a loss of reality, and the loss of possibilities of meaning and relationship. This is necessary for the return of love and affection, which further enables growth and development in a circular and continuing development.

Speaking in this way about maturation has the capacity to create arbitrary distinctions of maturation of affect and of spirituality. I have already spoken of the possibilities of their confusion. Spiritual identity is necessary as preparatory to celibacy. As it contains so it also focusses on identity. The spiritual identity can be 'other worldly' or by contrast 'world affirming'. The perspective of holiness, which is in the explanation and meaning attributed to our bodies and their relationship to society and to history, will vary accordingly. Peter Brown in his study of early Christian communities, perceived that their exercise of renunciation was an expression of mapping their freedom on their bodies:

> It had been connected with a heroic and sustained attempt, on the part of thinkers of widely different background and temper of mind, to map out the horizons of human freedom. The light of a great hope of future transformation glowed behind even the most austere statements of the ascetic position. To many continence had declared the end of the tyranny of the 'present age' ... In the words of John Chrysostom, 'Virginity made plain that ... the things of the resurrection stand at the door.' (Brown, 1988, 1 990: 442).

The universal perspectives of both spirituality and psycho-sexual development can be recognised in contemplation and compassion, where the individual views him or herself in and in relationship to a world. Asceticism is the total stance of the individual and not to be arbitrarily attached to any part of his or her life. The lines are drawn confusingly between the world which is public and the private world of the individual. Vows are made publicly and corporately but lives have also to be lived individually and privately. The difference between the two may vary considerably and create tension beyond expectation and experience. Unger has the useful expression of the tension as one existing between the desire for solidarity, and the simultaneous experience of thus being in jeopardy. N. O. Brown's argument for the recognition of the body between the drive theory, and through sublimation to culture is an expression of the organic in which these two worlds live:

> The death instinct is reconciled with the life instinct only in a life which is not repressed, which leaves no 'unlived lives' in the human body, the death instinct then being affirmed in a body which is willing to die. And, because the body is satisfied, the death instinct no longer drives it to change itself, and make history, and therefore, as Christian theology divined, its activity is in eternity. At the same time – and here again Christian theology and psychoanalysis agree – the resurrected body is the transfigured body, consciousness which does not negate any more (1970: 308).

What is 'affect' in terms of maturity. and available through the love of God (the spiritual life), and love of one another and in the particular, which is non-genital? As such it is aim inhibited. It is the language of friendship which is contributory to ongoing development as a life of both risk and responsibility. If any relationship evokes a sexual response it should not be abandoned for the fear of sexuality nor should celibacy become a strategy of avoidance. The significance of friendship is enshrined in the spiritual writings of St. Aelred of Rievaulx.

Maturation in the Religious Life defines, identity, intimacy, achievement and generativity, as focal developmental areas for the celibate. The maturation of affect develops within it an awareness of belonging. For those separated from their societies for particular reasons, belonging is their identification. It is the ground for intimacy. Belonging arises out of the mutual recognition of the individual and their community of each other, and the awareness of the commitment they have between them. The spiritual identity which is bound up in the personal identity and containing the sexual identity of a man or a woman, creates this possibility. This is intrapsychic as well: containing the dimensions of being both heterosexual and homosexual. Goergen says of the sexual identity:

> I will affirm that being celibate does not mean being asexual. Being celibate involves deeply that core of our being where we are not only with God and for God, but also with ourselves, our affectivity, genitality, femininity, masculinity. Heterosexuality, homosexuality, attractiveness. It is not a question of uprooting sexuality but of becoming sexual in a different way (1974. 1976: 88).

Achievement presides over identity and is given recognition in work or ministry. It is affirming and helps create an enduring identity. The necessity of generativity is in its contributing to the regeneration of the world around. It is present in the fostering of new generations; contributing to their own development and to the maintaining of our own developmental patterns and those of the world around us. It takes us into old age and asserts our responsibility for others of different generations. Intimacy is the growth of friendship in non-exploitative and intentional relationships for the development of self and with an awareness of body and eroticism. In celibacy this development is non-genital and affective and yet it is also important for an embodiment and physicality; contributing to the endopsychic imagery of ourselves and taking us beyond the boundaries of ourselves.

Through all this the Religious Life remains a life centred upon spiritual values.

Acceptance of faith and failure and the risks involved are necessary, even though the lifestyle is considered to be a life of perfection. This life must allow at all times for an understanding of guilt, but without allowing disgrace. Object relations will always be difficult though injuries can be minimised. Shame can be injurious and also inhibiting of reconciliation. Object relations is the meat of all people's lives and requires constant work and effort. They will never be easy or 'got right'. Rizutto (1979) has the lovely picture of the child having his or her pet God under their arm even before the possibility of an encounter with the God of tradition. Internal objects if they are not repressed, will be subject to change, and respond to a growth in faith.

Love leading to integration and restitution, creates new identities and further develops the identity that was able to begin the process. The constant shaping of new selves and the discarding of the old ones is a measure of this process of maturation. The ideals are redefined and reconstituted.

Friendship highlights the importance of the world of object relating in the maturational processes pertaining to the Religious Life:

> We may also observe that the effective operation of these opposite principles, like those of male and female, depends upon their reciprocity. Sexuality needs the disciplined austerity of the spirit in order to generate quality, while spirituality needs the primal fire of sex, for without this its products lack the penetrating vital flame. Hence the chastity which was so insisted upon by many of the medieval chroniclers was of an entirely different character from that enforced by respectability. Continence is the indispensable condition of individual achievement – not because sexuality is evil, but owing to the condition that the transformation of opposite elements can take place only when they are held in braced opposition (Baynes, 1940: 483).

Conclusions

> It takes indeed a healthy personality for the 'I' to be able to speak out of all these conditions in such a way that any given moment it can testify to a reasonably coherent self (Erikson 1968, 1983: 217).

The heart's desire, or more than the place of somatic experience, and also the place of psychic identity and subjectivity, requires an object to love or identify with. The choice of object(s) may be quite varied, and many in quantity. The object is only constituted as the self is constituted. There can be no other if there is no self. Their very existence depends upon one another. This perception rests upon the concept of narcissism, which is manifested through the pleasure principle, and the infant who is 'polymorphously perverse'. This narcissism as a reservoir of libido, contributes to self-gratification and other positive qualities of 'feeling good'. This is the ground for the religious experience of the numinous. The crucible of which is the mother infant matrix. For the religious, this is an expression of the ground from which arises revelation and the notion of grace or the experience of God.

To love beyond the toleration of ambivalence with the ability to tolerate dependency creates the environment for being in love and staying in love. A certain intrapsychic economy is required for this process to begin. Whether the Oedipal stage is the foundation of this environment and a necessary part of the equation is open to debate. It certainly contains the foundation that the person is loveable, and he or she knows that for further development in any maturational process love of another or others is required. It marks a distinction between being known as an object and being known as a subject, and knowing oneself as beloved.

The perception of a self provides an experience of being centred, as against being decentred, and being coherent, as opposed to incoherent. It contains the foundation for an identity with a capacity to make a choice of other objects. Every object choice has the potential to be a transitional object, which can be internalised and become the ground of creativity in transitional space. This may seem like a fusion of the object relations of Winnicott and the work of Edith Jacobson, and although drive theory and object relations might appear to be strange bedfellows it really signals where they can be related to one another. Through sexuality desire may be understood, though not always or necessarily gratified. Held, it is comprehended as the source of longing which can be creative and fertile. This is the embodiment of religious life and the creativity which gives expression to soul.

The self is an object of I. There is an essential axis between them. I may be able to integrate a number of selves at any particular time, to correlate paradox and reconcile contradiction. According to Juliet Mitchell this person is also subject invariably to an instability which represents the capacity for new identities and the emergence of new selves. The 'I', although called imaginal, is the person whom we address when we speak of our loneliness; or singularity. It is a reflection of the narcissism which is the basis for creativity. This aloneness can become loneliness, or it can become solitude. Of the two, the latter may be considered the healthier state. We can compare Winnicott's discussions of this in the capacity to be alone, and Bergmann's reflections on the capacity to be alone with our love objects. In both spheres the early mother child matrix, is important and primal.

Here I would clarify love objects as being distinct from sexual objects in interpersonal relationships. I recognise that we choose many different objects to relate to and to utilise, whether through desire or need. All these represent the wishes we contain. The incorporation of our relationships provides us with intrapsychic models, and the 'dramatis personae' of various experiences. It enables us to be both different according to the circumstances that we find ourselves in and to have an identity which is also consistent and enduring. The reasons for the choice of any particular object may not be immediately apparent. The choice may represent the resolution of internal conflict on the intrapsychic level perhaps reducing aggression, or expressing need and or receiving love and acceptance. The choice may also represent a transference with the compulsion to repeat, and may also be an attachment which is essential for psychical survival.

The Religious who has the capacity to 'love' has the capacity to deal with the relationships which are essential for affective maturing within and beyond his or her community. The Religious who is not capable of being in love will be promiscuous with his or her objects, and also vicariously live his or her life through the objects with which he or she surrounds themselves.

The selves which are contained in the 'I' and contribute to an enduring identity and relationship, are recreated and refurbished in that relationship. Although this is language which is particularly interpersonal and stresses the importance of this, it has an intrapsychic dimension, for those internal objects are adjusted and reordered according to new experiences. This dynamic enables object relations. Every self also has an endopsychic dimension, where he or she relates to his or her own psyche and soma with a continuing experience of an organic identity. For example a sexual self has knowledge of his or her genitals within the entire body and the expression of them which sustains that self.

Alternatively as affect is integrated, and new levels of development are attained, new psychic drives are observed differing from the earlier, primitive and basic drives. The desire for intimacy or achievement, or generativity, comes to be expressed developmentally. The basis of this expression in a sexual maturity with both its affective and genital aspects draws upon the ego ideal and its wishful self The spiritual identity expresses itself in the same way.

The Religious Life with its expression of singularity or solitariness through celibacy, and its concomitant as a worthwhile life must deal with the selves in a homosexual environment. This is Moorhouse's (1969) choice of term and the dilemma is one which he posed. The importance of sexual identity is as either man or woman, and then the understanding of each person's homosexuality and heterosexuality as though they represent part of a continuum is part of that identity. This is essential for a spiritual identity also and so the spiritual and sexual are interwoven. A man can be father, son, and brother. Alternatively for the Religious, he or she must learn independence with mature dependence. and the capacity to love beyond ambivalence. The questions of dominance and submission are bound up not only in the transference, but also in the commitment to the maintenance of personal and social matrices.

The endopsychic reality which I have called embodiment, deals not only with the individual but with his or her world, and the making of the distinction between them. There is a continuing dialogue between world and individual. In universal terms the psychoanalytical resolve with compassion and the spiritual with contemplation. He or she is an embodied mind in society, and has the experience of locomotor and ego-space and the experience of every other person's uniqueness and the need of and for the other. When mutually experienced the need of and for the other must result in a fruitful intercourse. It is a challenge to the Religious to find ways of being celibate without being sterile.

Bibliography

Allchin, A. M. (1983) *The Theology of the Religious Life: An Anglican Approach,* Oxford: SLG Press.

Altman, L. L. (1977) Some Vicissitudes of Love. *Journal of American Psa. Association* XXV: 35–52.

Ardetti, M. (1993) *The Celibate,* London: Sinclair-Stevenson.

Augustine, St. (1960) *The Confessions of St. Augustine,* London: Fontana.

Bailey, S. (1954) *Homosexuality and the Western Christian Tradition,* London: Longmans, Green and Co.

Balint, M. (1948) On Genital Love. In *Primary Love and Psychoanalytic Technique,* London: Hogarth Press and the Institute of Psycho-Analysis.
(1952) *Primary Love and Psychoanalytic Technique,* London: Tavistock.
(1968) *The Basic Fault,* London: Tavistock.

Baynes, H.G. (1940) *Mythology of the Soul,* London: Bailliere and Tindal Cox.

Beer, R.R. (1977) translated by Stern C. M., *Unicorn Myth and Reality,* London: Kery J. J.

Bergmann, M. S. (1971) Psychoanalytic Observations on the Capacity to Love. In *Separation. Individuation: Essays in*

Honour of Margaret S. Mahler. (eds McDevitt J. B. and Settlage C. F.), New York: International Universities Press.
(1980) On the Intrapsychic Function of Falling in Love. *Psychoanalytical Quarterly*, 49:56–77.
(1982) Platonic Love, Transference Love, and Love in Real Life. *Journal of the American Psycho-Analytical Association.* I :87–112.

Bernstein, M. (1976,1979) *Nuns,* New York: Bantam.

Bettelheim, B. (1991) *Freud and Man's Soul,* London: Penguin.

Boulding, M. (1982) *A Touch of God: Eight Monastic Journeys,* London: SPCK.

Brown, D & Pedder, J. (1979, 1991) *Introduction to Psychotherapy. An Outline of Psychodynamic Principles and Practice,* London: Tavistock Routledge.

Brown, J. A. C. (1991) *Freud and the Post-Freudians,* London: Penguin.

Brown, N. O. (1970) *Life Against Death. The Psychoanalytical Meaning of History,* New York: Wesleyan University Press.

Brown, P. (1990) *The Body and Society. Men, Women and Sexual Renunciation in Early Christianity,* Bungay: Faber and Faber.

Buttrick, G. A. et al. (1979) T*he Interpreters Bible in Twelve Volumes,* Nashville: Abingdon Press.

Corbin, H. (1977) *Spiritual Body and Celestial Earth.*

Translated from the French by Pearson, N., Princeton: Princeton University Press.

Cotter, J. (1977) The Gay Challenge to Traditional Notions of Human Sexuality. In *Towards a Theology of Gay Liberation.* (ed. By MacCourt, M.) London: SCM Press Ltd.

De Board, R. (1978) *The Psychoanalysis of Organizations: A Psychoanalytic Approach to Behaviour in Groups and Organisations,* London: Tavistock/Routledge.

Den Haag, E. (1964) Love or Marriage. In R. L. Coser. *The Family and its Structure and Functions,* London: St. Martin.

Dollimore, J. (1991) S*exual Dissidence. Augustine to Wilde, Freud to Foucault,* Oxford: Clarendon.

Elias, N. (1991) *The Society of Individuals,* Oxford: Basil Blackwell.

Elkin, A. P. (1977) *Aboriginal Men of High Degree,* St. Lucia: University of Queensland Press.

Erikson, E. H. (1968,1983) *Identity: Youth and Crisis,* London: Faber and Faber.
(1978) *Adulthood,* New York: W.W. Norton and Company.
(1959, 1980) *Identity and the Life Cycle,* New York: W.W. Norton and Company.
(1982) *The Life Cycle Completed. A Review,* New York: W.W. Norton and Company.

Erlande-Brandenburg, A. (1989) *La Dame a La Licorne,* Paris: Editions de la Reunion des Musees Nationaux.

Etchegoyen, R.H. (1991) *The Fundamemals/Psychoanalytic Technique*, London: H. Karnac

Friar, K. (1982) *Modern Greek Poetry*, Athens: P. Efstathiadis and Sons.

Foulkes, S. H. (1964) *Therapeutic Group Analysis*, London: George Allen and Unwin.

Freud, A. (1986) *The Ego and the Mechanisms of Defence*, London: The Hogarth Press.

Freud, S. (1900) *The Interpretation of Dreams*, Standard Edition. London: Hogarth Press.
(1905) *Three Essays on The Theory of Sexuality*, Penguin Library, Vol. 7: 1977, London: Penguin.
(1910) *Leonardo Da Vinci. A Memory of His Childhood.* London: Ark.
(1910) *Contributions to the Psychology of love I.* Standard Edition., London: Penguin.
(1912) On the Universal Tendency to Debasement, In *The Sphere of Love: Contributions to the Psychology of Love 2*, Standard Edition.
(1913) *Theme of the Three Caskets*, Standard Edition.
(1914) *On Narcissism.* Standard Edition.
(1915) *Instincts and Their Vicissitudes*, Standard Edition
(1918) *Contributions to the Psychology of Love, 3.* Standard Edition.
(1921) *Group Psychology and the Analysis of the Ego*, Standard Edition
(1923) *The Ego and the Id*, Standard Edition.

(1930) *Civilisation and its Discontents*, Standard Edition
(1940) *An Outline of Psychoanalysis.* Standard Edition.
(1974) *Two Short Accounts of Psycho Analysis: Five Lectures on Psycho Analysis, and the Question of Lay Analysis*, Harmondsworth: Penguin.
(1984) *On Metapsychology, The Theory of Psycho-analysis*, Harmondsworth: Penguin.

Glover, E. (1956) *On The Early Development of the Mind*, London: Imago.
(1968) *The Birth of the Ego. A Nuclear Hypothesis*, London: George Allen and Unwin.

Glyn, C. (1977) *A Mountain at the End of Night. Stories of Dream and Vision*, London: Victor Gollancz.

Goergen, D. (1974, 1976) *The Sexual Celibate*, London: SPCK.

Gramick, J. (ed.) (1989) *Homosexuality in the Priesthood and the Religious Life*, New York: Crossroad.

Greeley, Andrew M. (1975, 1984) *Love and Play*, London: W. H. Allen.

Grosskurth, P. (1989) *Melanie Klein*, London: Karnac.

Guntrip, H (1977) *Personality structure and Human Interaction. The Developing Synthesis of Psychodynamic Theory*, London: Hogarth.
(1968) Spirituality and Psychology. In *Spirituality for Today: From Papers from the 1967 Parish and People Conference.* (ed. James, E.) London: SCM.

(1986) *Schizoid Phenomena. Object Relations and the Self.* London: Hogarth Press.

Hanley, C. & Lazarowitz, M. (eds.) (1970) *Psychoanalysis and Philosophy*, New York: International Universities Press.

Helman, C. (1991) *Body Myths*, London: Chatto and Windus.

Hillman, J. (1992) *The Thought of the Heart and the Soul of the World*, Dallas, Texas: Spring Books.

Holmes, J. (1993) People and Places. Bridges to Borderlines. The Bridge Foundation Conference on Borderline Personality Disorder, Bristol, November 1992. *Psychiatric Bulletin*, 17: 238–239.

Hopper, E. (1991) Encapsulation as a Defence Against the Fear of Annihilation. *International Journal of Psycho-Analysis*, 72: 607.

Jacobson, E. (1965) *The Self and the Object World*, London: Hogarth Press.

(1967) *Psychotic Conflict and Reality*, New York: The New York Psychoanalytic Institute and the Hogarth Press.

(1977) *Depression: Comparative Studies of Normal, Neurotic and Psychotic Conditions*, New York: International Universities Press.

Jung, C. G. (1959,1969) *Mandala Symbolism*, translated by Hull, R. F. C. From *The Collected works of C. G. Jung, Volume 9: Part I*, Bollingen Series XX, Princeton: Princeton University Press.

(1958, 1969, 1977) *Psychology and Religion: East and West*, translated by Hull, R. F. C. From *The Collected Works of C. G. Jung, Vol. 11*, Bollingen Series XX. Princeton: Princeton University Press.

Kenel, M. E. (1986) A Celibate's Sexuality and Intimacy. *Human Development*, Vol 7(1): 14–19.

Kerenyi, K & Hillman, J. (1991) *Oedipus Variations. Studies in Literature and Psychoanalysis*, Dallas: Spring Publications.

Kernberg, O. (1977) Boundaries and Structures in Love Relations. *Journal of the American Psychoanalytic Association*, 25:81–114.
(1992) *Aggression in Personality Disorders and Peversions*, New York: Yale University Press.

Laplanche, J. & Pontalis, J. B. (1988) *The Language of Psychoanalysis*, London: Karnac Books and The Institute of Psycho-analysis.

Lasky, J. F. & Silverman, H. W. (1988) Editors. *Love: Psychoanalytic Perspectives*, New York: New York University Press.

Le Clerq, J. (1978) *The Love/Learning and the Desire for God: A Study of Monastic Culture*, London: SPCK.

Leeson, E. (ed.) (1980) *The New Golden Treasury of English Verse*, Macmillan: London.

Liddell, H. G. & Scott, R. (1856) *A Lexicon. Abridged from the Greek-English Lexicon*, Oxford: Oxford University Press.

Liddon, S. C. (1989) *The Dual Brain, Religion and the Unconscious,* Buffalo, New York: Prometheus.

Lightfoot, J. B. (1891,1907) The Shepherd of Hermas. In Harmer, J. R. (ed.) *The Apostolic Fathers,* London: MacMillan

Loewald, H. (1978) *Psychoanalysis and the History of the Individual,* New Haven: Yale University Press.

Loudon, M. (1992) *Unveiled. Nuns Talking.* London: Chatto and Windus.

MacCary, W. Thomas. (1982) *Childlike Achilles, Ontogeny and Phylogeny in the Iliad,* New York: Columbia Press.

Macourt, Malcolm (1977) *Towards a Theology of Gay Liberation,* London: SCM Press Ltd.

McDargh, J. (1983) *Psycho-Analytic Object Relations Theory and the Study of Religion,* London: University Press of America.

McDevitt, J. B. & Settlage, C. F. (eds) (1971) *Separation. Individuation: Essays in Honour of Margaret S. Mahler.* New York: International Universities Press.

McDougall, J. (1989) *Theaters of the Body, A Psycho-analytic Approach to Psychosomatic Illness,* London: W.W. Norton. (1990) *Plea for a Measure of Abnormality,* London: Free Association.

Mahler, M., Pine, F. & Bergman, A. (1991) *The Psychological Birth of the Human Infant,* London: Karnac Books and the Maresfield Library.

Maitland, S. (1984,1993) *Virgin Territory*, London: Virago.

Marteau, L. (1983) *Coming Together: A Psychological Reflection on the Religious Life*, Mill Hill, London: T. Shand Publications.
(1986) *Existential Short Term Therapy*, London: The Dympa Centre.

Massie, H. R. & Rosenthal, J. (1984) *Childhood Psychosis in the First Four Years of Life*. Baskerville: McGraw-Hill Book Company.

Masterson, J. F. (1981) *The Narcissistic and Borderline Disorders. An Integrated Developmental Approach*. New York: Brunner/Mazel

Meissner, W. W., S. J. (1992) *The Psychology of a Saint. Ignatius of Loyola*, New Haven: Yale University Press.

Merton, T. (1977) *The Monastic Journey*, London: Sheldon Press.

Mitchell, J. (ed.) (1986) *The Selected Melanie Klein*, London: Penguin.
(1990) *Psychoanalysis and Feminism*, London: Penguin.

Moore, T. (ed.) (1989, 1990) T*he Essential James Hillman. A Blue Fire*. London: Routledge.

Moorhouse, G. (1969) *Against All Reason*, London: Sceptre.

Nelson, J.B. (1979) *Embodiment*, Philadelphia: Westminster Press.
(1988) *Between Two Gardens*, New York: The Pilgrim Press.

(1988) *The Intimate Connection: Male Sexuality, Masculine Spirituality*, Philadelphia: Westminster Press.
(1992) *Body Theology*, Louisville: Westminster & John Knox Press.
(1993) Varied Meanings of Marriage and Fidelity. In Scott K. & Warren, M. (eds) *Perspectives on Marriage. A Reader*, New York; Oxford University Press.

Orchard, G. (1993) Celibacy: A Singular Freedom. From *Intimacy and Sexuality*. The Christian Action Journal of Summer 1993, London: Christian Action, St. Anselm's Church Hall, Kennington Cross.

Ogden, T. H. (1990) *The Matrix of the Mind. Object Relations and the Psychoanalytic Dialogue*, Northvale, New Jersey: Jason Aronson Inc.

Owen, I. R. (1993) On Desire: Its Development and Some Clinical Examples. *British Journal of Medical Psychology* 66: 229–238, Great Britain: The British Psychological Society.

Parry, D. (1980) *Households of God. The Rule of St. Benedict*, London: Darton, Longman and Todd.

Pearson, G. (1975) *The Deviant Imagination. Psychiatry, Social Work and Social Change*, London: MacMillan.

Pemberton, C. (1993) More Thoughts on Revisioning. From *Encounter and Exchange*, Bulletin No. 65 January 1993. St.Mary's Convent, Freeland, Witney United Kingdom: The Journal of the Communities' Consultative Council of the Church of England.

Pines, M. (ed.) (1985) *Bion and Group Psychology*, International Library of Group Psychology and Group Process, London: Routledge and Kegan Paul.

Ranke-Heinemann, U. (1988, 1990) *Eunuchs or Heaven, the Catholic Church and Sexuality*, translated by John Brownjohn, London: Andre Deutsch.

Rayner, E. (1990) *The Independent Mind in British Psychoanalysis*, London: Free Association.

Rickman, J. M.D. (1957) Compiled by W. C. M. Scott, *Selected Contributions to Psycho-analysis*, London: The Hogarth Press and the Institute of Psycho-analysis.

Ricoeur, P. (1970) translated by Denis Savage, *Freud and Philosophy: An Essay on Interpretation*, Yale: Yale University Press.

Ritvo, S. M. (1971) Margaret Mahler: Scientist, Psychoanalyst and Teacher. In *Separation. Individuation: Essays in Honour of Margaret S. Mahler*, McDevitt, J. B. & Settlage, C. F. (eds) New York: International Universities Press.

Rizzuto, A-M., MD (1979) *The Birth of the Living God: A Psychoanalytic Study*, Chicago: University of Chicago Press.

Roberts, J.P. (1982) Foulkes' Concept of the Matrix, *Group Analysis* 15(2): 11–26.

Roberts, J. & Pines, M. (eds) (1991) *The Practice of Group Analysis*, London: Tavistock/Routledge.

Rose, J. (1991) *Sexuality in the Field of Vision,* London: Verso.

Sammon, S. D. (1993) *An Undivided Heart. Making Sense of Celibate Chastity,* New York: Alba House.

Samuels, A. (ed.) (1985) *The Father: Contemporary Jungian Perspectives,* London: Free Association Books.
(1989) *The Plural Psyche. Personality, Morality and the Father,* London: Routledge.
(1989) (ed.) *Psychopathology. Contemporary Jungian Perspectives,* London: Karnac.
(1986) with Shorter, B. & Plaut, F. *A Critical Dictionary of Jungian Analysis,* London: Routledge and Kegan Paul plc.

Sandison, R. (1993) The Presence of God in the Group, *Group Analysis,* 26(1): 55–65.

Sandler, J. & Freud, A. (1985) *The Analysis of Defense; The Ego and the Mechanisms of Defence Revisited,* New York: International Universities Press.

Sartre, J-P. (1985) *Sketch for a Theory of Emotions,* London: Methuen

Sayers, J. (1991) *Mothering Psychoanalysis,* London: Hamish Hamilton.

Schlachet, B.C. & B. Waxenberg (1988) What is This Thing Called Love? The Popular Ballad as a Framework for Changing Conceptions of Love. From *Love: Psychoanalytic Perspectives,* Lassky J. F. & Silverman, H. W. (eds) New York: New York University Press

Schneiders, S. M. (1986) *New Wineskins. Re-imagining Religious Life Today*, New York: Paulist Press.

Schwartz-Salant, N. (1982) *Narcissism and Character Transformation*, Toronto: Inner City Books.

Silverman, H. W. (1988) Aspects of the Erotic Transference. From *Love: Psychoanalytic Perspectives*, Lassky J. F. & Silverman, H. W. (eds) New York: New York University Press

Sinason, V. (1992) *Mental Handicap and the Human Condition*, London: Free Association.

Sipress, L. (1974) *The Unicorn Tapestries*. Adapted from the study by Margaret B. Freeman, New York: The Metropolitan Museum of Art.

Smelser, N. & Erikson E. (1980) *Themes of Work and Love in Adulthood*, London Grant McIntyre.

Snidle, H. (1992) Celibacy: The Need for Friendship. From The Revd. A. W. Evans (ed) at al. *Advent/Adfent*, An Occasional. Publication. Penarth CF62EX: The Church in Wales Board of Mission. The Division For Social Responsibility.

Stevens, A. (1990,1991) *On Jung*, London: Penguin.

Symington, N. (1990) *The Analytic Experience. Lectures from the Tavistock*, London: Free Association.
(1993) *Narcissism: A New Theory*, London: Karnac.

Traheme, T. (1927) *Centuries of Meditations*, London: Dobell.

Thomas, G. (1986) *Desire and Denial. Sexuality and Vocation: A Church in Crisis*, London: Grafton Books.

Turner, B. S. (1984,1989) *The Body and Society. Explorations in Social Theory*, Oxford: Basil Blackwell.

Unger, R. M. (1984) *Passion, an Essay on Personality*, New York: Free Press.

Van der Kleij, G. (1993) Religion and Freud and Groups. *Group Analysis* 26(1): 27–37.

Voillaume, R. (1978) *Fallow Me*, London: Darton, Longman and Todd.

Waelder, R. (1930) The Principle of Multiple Function: Observations on Over Determination. *The Psycho Analytical Quarterly* 5(1): 45–62.

Ward, B. (1987) *Harlots of the Desert: A Study of Repentance in Early Monastic Sources*, London: Mowbray

Wescott, B. (1993) Group Analysis and Religion: Is there a Common Ground? Ideas arising from the Paper by Gregory Van der Kleij, *Group Analysis* 26(1): 39–53.

Weeks, J. (1985) *Sexuality and its Discontents: Meaning and Myths of Modern Sexualities*, London: Routledge and Kegan Paul.

Wilber, K. (1979, 1981) *No Boundary, Easter and Western Approaches to Personal Growth*, London: Shambala.

Winnicott, D. W. (1984) *The Child, The Family, and The Outside World*, Harmondsworth: Pelican.

(1986) *Home is Where We Start From*, New York and London: W.W. Norton and Company.

(1988) *Human Nature*, London: Free Association Books

(1989) *Psycho-analytic Explorations*, London: Karnac.

Wisdom, J. 0. (1970) Freud and Melanie Klein: Psychology, Ontology and Weltanschaaung. In Hanley, C. & Lazarowitz. M. *Psycho-Analysis and Philosophy*, New York: International Universities Press.

Acknowledgements

I am indebted to my friend Christina Rees CBE for her inspiration to write this section.

I am blessed by membership in the Society of Saint Francis and all its provinces, for their kindness and guidance has directed me to this opportunity.

I am extremely grateful for the guiding hand of Dr Rosemary Barnard in the overseeing of the writing of this manuscript, when I came back to Australia from a time way in another world.

It would not have been possible to bring this manuscript to fruition if I had not had the wise hand of Dr Jeff Roberts of the Royal London Hospital as my mentor, and by my side. I functioned there as an honorary psychotherapist and took his faith in the processes of the Group Analytic Society, while I was studying for a master's degree of the Psychology of Therapy and Counselling

Whilst in London I was tended graciously in residence by the Nursing Sisters of Saint John the Divine in Vauxhall London and saw into their world. I was especially grateful the for the work of Sr Eva Heyman RSJ who gave me insight into a world of sexuality and religious life as a reality together and tested my world of love.

I also remember those who have treated me graciously well

and respectfully, wherein I have trod this path faithfully, and I have moved on to a world of poetry which is now my inspiration for writing. My mother encouraged me to write.

I have since created my world of writing through a master's degree of Creative Writing at Sydney University, and especially I register my thanks to Associate-Professor Kate Lilley, who understood my mind and its processes and guided me in the utmost.

I give thanks for Thor Blomfield and Matthew Egan always at my side in these latter days – and it was the guiding mind of Dr Michael Williamson psychotherapist of The Black Dog Institute who helped me sew together the disparate parts of my processes and took me into the freehold world of being a poet, and I am delighted he will launch this book.

About the Author

Noel Jeffs SSF is an Anglican Friar originally from Gippsland, Australia. He is a sometimes student of Kate Lilley and others for a Master of Creative Writing at Sydney University. He is a disabled person living alone who enjoys conversations and silence and writing. Noel has a master's degree in Mental Health and has trained as a psychotherapist.

His poetry print publication *Under the Dome* is still available from Garden Lounge in Newton, Sydney. He has been published in Burrows twice and is currently part of two anthologies, David Reuters' *Outer Space/Inner Minds* and *Antologie Romana Australiana,* a cross-cultural work of dialogue and discourse between his Sydney workshop and the 'Palatul Culturii Bistrita-Romania' where he was translated into Romanian.

He is currently also working on the manuscript of his thesis poems *Walking in Stealth* in preparation for release as a print publication, now that he has made this manuscript, *Maturing in the Religious Life,* available to a wider audience.

www.ingramcontent.com/pod-product-compliance
Ingram Content Group UK Ltd.
Pitfield, Milton Keynes, MK11 3LW, UK
UKHW020423250726
13967UKWH00007B/2788